Excellent Courses
A Culinary Legacy of Ravenscroft

RAVENSCROFT

Excellent Courses
A Culinary Legacy of Ravenscroft

Published by Ravenscroft School, Inc.

Copyright © 2008 by
Ravenscroft School, Inc.
7409 Falls of Neuse Road
Raleigh, North Carolina 27615
919-847-0900
http://excellentcourses.ravenscroft.org

Cover and chapter opener concepts: Debra Turner
Graphic design: Debra Turner Graphic Design
Front cover, back cover, chapter opener, and title page photography: Chris Watters
Front matter spread photography: Gonet Gateway, Susan Washburn;
Robert P. Holding, Jr. Memorial Garden, Chris Watters; Lower School Butterfly Garden,
Susan Washburn; Cherry Blossom, Jack Morton '96; Murphy Bell Tower in Snow, Jack Morton '96;
Ravenscroft Stadium, Susan Washburn; Murphy Family Arboretum, Diane Schaff;
young peoples' theatre, Chris Watters; Middle & Upper School Library, Susan Washburn;
Graduation, Jack Morton '96

ISBN: 978-0-615-17649-9

Edited, Designed, and Produced by
CommunityClassics™
An imprint of

a wholly owned subsidiary of Southwestern/Great American, Inc.
P. O. Box 305142
Nashville, Tennessee 37230
800-358-0560

Manufactured in the United States of America
First Printing: 2008
4,000 copies

All proceeds benefit Ravenscroft and its outreach programs.

A Message from the Head of School

There is something quite wonderful about a well-trained, confident cook who can prepare a meal which nourishes the soul as well as the body. The ability to create, prepare, and serve others is an important skill passed down from parent to child. The kitchen is at the heart of many homes where conversations are shared, traditions are born, and beautiful memories are lasting.

Thanks to the tremendous effort of a dedicated group of parent volunteers, we can all get back to our kitchens to try out these wonderful recipes shared by our community members. This cookbook is a valuable gift to and from our community. Through it, we can prepare good meals for our families and create opportunities to listen, learn, and teach—which, of course, is what we do best at Ravenscroft. Enjoy this special treasure!

Sincerely,
DOREEN C. KELLY
HEAD OF SCHOOL

A picture is worth a thousand words. This cookbook is graced with exceptional photography, especially on the cover and on the opening page of each recipe section. Exquisite "tablescapes" were created to capture and convey the depth and range of Ravenscroft School's activities, programs, and traditions. Each item, hand-selected and meticulously placed by the design committee, represents something unique or important to our community. The violin symbolizes the School's commitment to the Fine Arts for all ages, including violin instruction as part of the core curriculum for all Ravenscroft Kindergarten students. The long-stemmed yellow rose calls to mind the tradition of each senior presenting a yellow rose to his or her mother at graduation. The globe suggests the School's ties to the international community, with students from over 20 countries represented each year in our enrollment. There are like reasons for every item. *Excellent Courses* is grateful to Dr. Christopher Watters for his stunning photography and for the many hours spent with the design committee capturing the rich and vibrant spirit of Ravenscroft in all of its seasons.

Tobacco Road Cellars

"Excellent Courses is proud to select the best boutique winery in California to pair with our menus."

Tobacco Road Cellars is honored to partner with *Excellent Courses*. To experience our world-class Cabernet Sauvignon, Pinot Noir, and Syrah and to learn more about our exclusive Regency Club, visit www.tobaccoroadcellars.com.
    —Jason Earnest & Dusty Field, Co-Founders

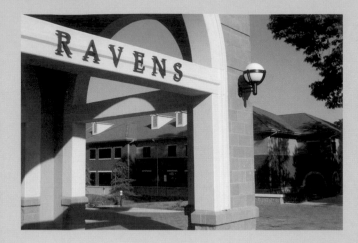

Ravenscroft School

Table of Contents

FOREWORD PAGE 7

A BRIEF HISTORY OF RAVENSCROFT SCHOOL PAGE 8

SPONSORS OF *EXCELLENT COURSES* PAGE 10

EXCELLENT COURSES COMMITTEE MEMBERS PAGE 11

CONTRIBUTORS PAGE 12

BACK TO SCHOOL PAGE 14

CELEBRATIONS PAGE 64

WINTER WARMTH PAGE 98

SPRING BREAK PAGE 132

GRADUATION PAGE 182

RESTAURANT RECIPE CONTRIBUTORS PAGE 232

INDEX PAGE 233

ORDER INFORMATION PAGE 240

Ravenscroft's formal school crest adorns recipes with a special place in our school history.

A Word about Excellent Courses

The renowned French chef George Blanc has said: "Happy and successful cooking doesn't rely only on know-how; it comes from the heart, makes great demands on the palate and needs enthusiasm and a deep love for food to bring it to life." When a small group of parent volunteers undertook the creation of a Ravenscroft School cookbook in the spring of 2007, we found Chef Blanc's words particularly apt to describe the process upon which we had embarked. We probably possessed more enthusiasm than know-how, but we all shared both a love for good food and a profound appreciation of the outstanding school to which we had entrusted our children's education. As the project evolved, we also found that the demands of the work were more than offset by the rewards of sharing and friendship.

From the beginning, we envisioned crafting a cookbook that would not only showcase our best recipes, but also capture the essence of who we are, the Ravenscroft community. Our history, relationships, and traditions are at the core of our community, and they are woven through these pages with a sense of genuine affection and pride. The book is organized by seasons. Like the school year, it begins with fall and ends with summer, a passage that invites reflection, discovery, and growth.

Excellent Courses, A Culinary Legacy of Ravenscroft is a reality because of the tireless efforts and commitment of dedicated volunteers. Every page reflects the extraordinary talents of the committee members who produced this culinary treasure, and I am thankful for their time, energy, creativity, and constant willingness to "go the extra mile." In addition, the book would not have been possible without the involvement and support of the Ravenscroft Parents' Association, the School's administration, and the Ravenscroft community as a whole. We received over five hundred recipes from families, alumni, faculty, and friends of the School. Countless hours of organizing, testing, tasting, editing, and proofreading went into each recipe and into the creation of the delectable seasonal menus contained in this volume. Like Ravenscroft, Excellent Courses, is just that—excellent. Its tried-and-true recipes represent our very best. We hope they will become favorites for you and your family and friends throughout the seasons in all the years to come.

SHERRI CASS
EXCELLENT COURSES COMMITTEE CHAIR
March 2008

A Brief History of Ravenscroft School

(Adapted from Ravenscroft School: Story of a Southern School by Susan Ehtesham-Zedeh)

Ravenscroft began as the Parish school of Christ Episcopal Church in Raleigh, North Carolina. Founded in 1862 through a bequest in the will of Dr. Josiah Watson, a physician and prominent North Carolina statesman, the School officially opened its doors in 1868. It was housed in a humble wooden frame building on the north side of Christ Church facing Capitol Square in downtown Raleigh, and later in the Parish house of St. Savior's Chapel at Johnson and West Streets. The School was active until 1912, but there is no record of its operation after that date until 1937, when the Vestry of Christ Church authorized funds to revive the Parish School. The Vestry chose the name Ravenscroft School to honor the Right Reverend John Stark Ravenscroft, the first Bishop of the Episcopal Diocese of North Carolina (1823–1830) and first Rector of Christ Church.

The Right Reverend John Stark Ravenscroft

On September 13, 1937, Ravenscroft School opened its doors to 135 students in grades K–5 at the Parish House of St. Savior's Chapel on Tucker Street. It was at the Tucker Street campus, where the School would remain for more than thirty years, that its character as a caring and close-knit community was really established. Students of that era recall the dedication and leadership of teachers and staff and the warm, family feeling that prevailed. The Ravenscroft community, including parents, the Church, and a dynamic Board of Trustees, banded together to provide the support necessary for the School to thrive.

In February of 1966 a committee calling itself the "Friends of Ravenscroft" accepted full responsibility for operating the School. It was the vision, drive, and determination of these leaders, along with that of administrators, parents, members of the Board of Trustees, and other supporters that transformed Ravenscroft from a Parish school to a dynamic, nonsectarian, independent academic institution. The overwhelming generosity of the School's supporters allowed the Board of Trustees to purchase the current 115-acre campus on Falls of the Neuse Road in 1968.

Ravenscroft has continued to grow, both physically and in its stature as a leader in academic excellence. The School has achieved this status by nurturing the individual potential of its students and by preparing them to thrive in a complex and interdependent world; by striving for diversity in its student body and for innovation in all of its programs; and by grounding its values in the effort to embrace community and to foster collective growth. With these ideals as the foundation for its future, Ravenscroft School is certain to continue its legacy of excellence for many years to come.

Ravenscroft School, Tucker Street Campus

The history of Ravenscroft School is, at its core, a story of the people whose vision, drive, dedication, and generosity have combined throughout the years to create a unique environment for learning, where each student is challenged to discover his or her highest potential and to strive toward excellence in all aspects of life. It is the story of generations of students, teachers, parents, administrators, friends, and benefactors who have worked together, sometimes in the face of daunting odds, to create not only the preeminent academic institution that Ravenscroft has become, but also the close-knit community which is at the heart of the School's mission and success.

Sponsors of Excellent Courses

Gold Sponsors

Ravenscroft Board of Trustees

Launch Party Hosts

Jan and Peter Brown
Sherri and Robb Cass
Jackie and Tom Clare
Sarah and Bill ('80) Cozart
Pam ('63) and T. Barker ('61) Dameron
Laura and Mark Davidson
Wynn and James Dorsett
Angie and Rick Dowd
Rose and Duke ('76) Finley
Genevieve and Bill Francis
Sallie ('81) and John Glover
Kim and Kenny Hammerstein
Ann and Fallon Hanley
Reah and Keith Kittelberger
Charlene and Bill Knape
Sara and Andrew May
Lonnie and Joey McNeill
Donna and Lee Morris
Gretchen and Ben Pratt
Jan and Munther Qubain
Jane and Michael Reed
Ellen and Jeff Werner
Liza and Joel ('85) Williams
Mary Clark and Erwin Williams
Flo and Charles ('47) Winston
Jenny and Charles ('78) Winston, Jr.
Tracy and Bob ('80) Winston

Special Event Hosts

Martha and Ken Howard
Sara and Andrew May

Photography

Chris Watters

Graphic Design

Debra Turner Graphic Design

Friends of Excellent Courses

Anonymous
Stephanie and Bill Anderson
Carrie and Chris Antonello
Nancy and Jose Armstrong
Darlene and Rick Brajer
Romy and Player Barefoot
Mary Grady ('81) and Vic ('74) Bell
Cathy and Ed Byman
Judi and Joe Call
Carol Cass
Fairley Bell ('77) and Dan Cook
Barbara and Skipper ('79) Day
Wynn and James Dorsett
Margaret and Rans Douglas
Sarah Wesley Fox ('73) and Craig Wheaton
Jennie and Wilson Hayman
Christine Rogers and Stephen Hollis
Chris and Baker Jackson
Doreen and Chris Kelly
Pam and David Kirkbride
Patti and James Ledyard
Kerry and John Malitoris
Elizabeth and Tom Manley
Sally and Bill Moore
Mary and Bill ('74) Moss
Kristin and John Replogle
Fran and Watson ('38) Pugh
Lisa and Michael Sandman
Marian ('74) and Billy ('73) Troxler
Ward's Fruit & Produce Company
Wendy Bird Interiors

Excellent Courses Committee Members

Chairperson

Sherri Cass

Recipe Collection

Ellen Werner, Chairperson
Nancy Armstrong
Christine Finney
Kim Gridley
Shelly Sanders
Doreen Silver
Michelle Strong
Sheri Timmons
Liza Williams
Mimi Zaytoun

Menu Development

Ellen Werner

Kitchen Testing/Tasting

Kim Hammerstein, Chairperson
Lonnie McNeill
Jane Reed

Design

Laura Kay Berry, Chairperson
Fran Buckley
Cathy Hirsch
Donna Miller
Debra Turner

Marketing

Donna Morris

Historical Content

Martha Howard
Elizabeth Manley

Special Events

Liza Williams
Mary Clark Williams

Finance

Gretchen Pratt
Pamela Price

Proofing

Laura Davidson
Jan Qubain

Data Entry

Jane Reed

PA Co-Presidents

2006–07 Laura Davidson & Jan Qubain
2007–08 Jackie Clare & Ann Hanley
2008–09 Pam Dameron ('63) & Wynn Dorsett

Contributors

Excellent Courses wishes to sincerely thank the following persons for their contributions to this culinary legacy. Each person is valued for submitting or testing recipes that appear in this cookbook. We regret, due to limited space, not all recipes could be printed.

Sherry Adams	Kristin Chapman	B. J. Frey
Trey Adams	Jackie Clare	Aniko Gaal
Margaret Ajac	Beth Collawn	Paula Gale
Alicia Alford	James Collawn, M.D.	Marynell Gehrke
Terri Allen	Michelle Connell	Susan Toney Gilliam
Stephanie Anderson	Mimi Cook	Caroline Gilly
Carol Andrews	Joy Cooper	Caline Glenn
Angus Barn	Sarah Cozart	Ann Gozzo
Carrie Antonello	Margaret M. Cress	Kim Gridley
Nancy Armstrong	Andrea Crumpton	Susy Guilford
Laura Kay Berry	Pam Dameron ('63)	Laura Gulden
Alex Bireline	Martine Davis	Kim Hammerstein
Laurie Blizzard	Barbara Day	Ann Hanley
Mary Bossong	Susan DeJoy	Jennie Hayman
Cathy Bowen	Karen Dillinger	Blaze Hillman
Mary Craig Brown	Wynn Dorsett	Phyllis Hinson
Sue Brown	Vicki Eackles-Oehling	Cathy Hirsch
Elena Burns	Rose Finley	Mary Sue Hitch
Judy Cartret-Jenkins	Christine Finney	Holden's Barbecue
Carol Cass	P. G. ('40) & Ann Fox	Chris Johnson ('74)
Sherri Cass	Pam Freeman ('88)	Esther V. Jones

Robbin King	Jan Qubain	Jean Stephano
Reah Kittelberger	Delores Quesenberry	Jackie Stocks
Pam Koziel	Darby Quirk	Jane Story
Mary-Beth Lindenmuth	Susan Ramquist	Carolyn Stradley
Kerry Malitoris	Maria Ramusevic	Michelle Strong
Tal Mangum ('77)	Leslie Rankin	Nancy (Pickel) Tannenbaum
Elizabeth Manley	Gayle Rasberry	Melanie Tharrington
Jennifer Marchi	Debbie Ratliff	Myrtle Tharrington
Sara May	Jane Reed	Sheri Timmons
Mindy McDowell	Renee Riggs	Yesim Tomac
Linda McGhee	Lisa Russo	Debra Turner
Caryn McNeill	Laura Ryan	Rana Van Name
Elizabeth Melvin ('76)	Juliet Sadd	Tina Vorhees
Sally M. Moore	Lisa Sandman	Susan Washburn
Donna Morris	Mary Santos	Ginny Watters
Kris Morton	Carver Sapp ('68)	Julia Wells
Sigrid Morton	Diane Schaaf	Ellen Werner
Diane Murphy	Sue Scheier	Darlene Wilkins
Steve Murphy	Debbie Schofield	Liza Williams
Diane Norwood	Second Empire	Mary Clark Williams
Linda Nunnallee	Doreen Silver	Jenny Winston
Debbie Pirotte	Rusine Sinclair	Winston's Grille
Stephanie Poole	Tammy Squires	Prudence Woo
Abby Presson	Micki Stall	Mimi Zaytoun

Contributors 13

Fall comes to the Ravenscroft campus with an air of excitement and anticipation. The return to school marks a season of new beginnings, a time to create and to explore, when every day seems to offer a sense of possibility. In Lower School classrooms, eager children find reassurance in the welcoming smiles of teachers. They master new lessons with enthusiasm and embrace the structure of predictable routines. Older students set new goals for success, resolving to meet the challenges of the year ahead while still enjoying time with friends. As August quickly fades into the golden days of September and beyond, the campus is alive with activity and high expectations.

Fall is also a time of gathering, when the Ravenscroft community comes together for a variety of traditional activities: the flag-raising ceremony on the first day of school; Fall Festival with its activities, games, and family fun; and the Book Fair, a special favorite of children and parents alike. Perhaps most exciting in the minds of students are gatherings for fall athletic events. School spirit rises to great heights, especially for Homecoming, when old friendships are rekindled, new memories are made, and Ravens of all generations remember that you can go home again.

Our "Back to School" recipes capture the many moods of a North Carolina fall. Seasonal soups and salads reflect the bounty of the harvest. Main courses and side dishes offer an assortment of flavors and textures appropriate for warm days and cooler nights. And from Savory Southern Biscuits to Old-Fashioned Pecan Pie, there are autumn breads and desserts to satisfy a range of tastes. Whether you are preparing a simple family meal or planning an elegant dinner party, these delicious recipes will bring a sense of excitement and anticipation to your own gatherings in this season of new beginnings.

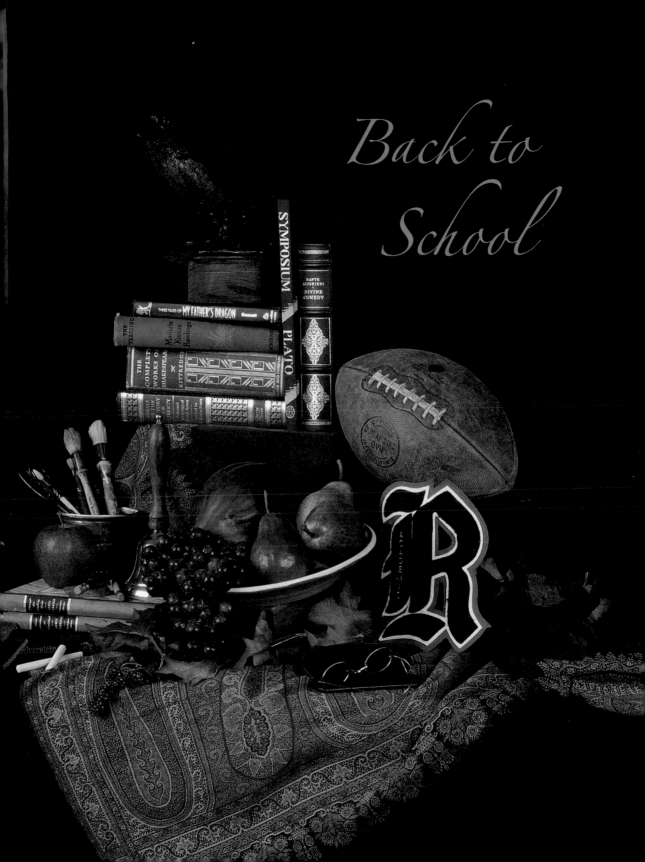

Back to

School

Chapter Index

Mushroom Shallot Quiche

Country Ham Rolls

French Toast Strata with Cider Syrup

Savory Southern Biscuits

Sweet Potato Angel Biscuits

Pumpkin Apple Streusel Muffins

Marinated Vegetable Platter

Spicy Pimento Cheese

Savory Chicken Crescents

Empanadas

Sausage-Stuffed Mushrooms

Scallops in Champagne Saffron Sauce

Beef and Sausage Chili

Vegetarian Bean Chili

Tailgate Corn Chowder

Baked Onion Soup

Sausage Tortellini Soup

Napa Cabbage Salad

Caesar Salad

Spinach, Apple and Bacon Salad

Roasted Chicken Salad

Chicken Salad with Blue Cheese and
    Dried Cherries

Mediterranean Pasta Salad

Flank Steak in Wine Sauce

Winston's Grille Meat Loaf

Gingered Pork Tenderloin

Tuscan Grilled Pork

Sausage-Stuffed Acorn Squash

Greek Chicken Breasts

Spicy Oven-Fried Chicken

Spanish Fish

Baked Seafood Salad

Easy Shrimp Pasta

Italian Vegetable Lasagna

Garlic Broccoli

Rosemary Spoon Bread

Wild Mushroom Bread Pudding

Kale with Roasted Red Peppers and Olives

Chocolate Layer Cake

Pumpkin Pound Cake with
    Brown Sugar Glaze

Molasses Bars

Cheesy Apple Dapple Squares

Cowboy Cookies

Ginger Bends

Cranberry Tart

Old-Fashioned Pecan Pie

Sour Cream Apple Pie

Baked Pears with Blue Cheese and Port

Back to School

Menus

Picnic at the Lake

Spicy Pimento Cheese

Roasted Chicken Salad Sandwiches

Mediterranean Pasta Salad

Cheesy Apple Dapple Squares

Football Tailgate

Tailgate Corn Chowder

Country Ham Rolls

Spicy Oven-Fried Chicken

Napa Cabbage Salad

Molasses Bars

Cowboy Cookies

2006 Tobacco Road Syrah, Santa Barbara

Do-Ahead Halloween Dinner

Beef and Sausage Chili

Savory Southern Biscuits

Pumpkin Pound Cake with
Brown Sugar Glaze

Elegant Fall Dinner

Scallops in Champagne Saffron Sauce

Spinach, Apple & Bacon Salad

Tuscan Grilled Veal Chops

Wild Mushroom Pudding

Baked Pears with Blue Cheese and Port

*2006 Tobacco Road Cabernet Sauvignon
"The Tradition," Napa Valley*

Neighborhood Potluck

Marinated Vegetable Platter

Italian Vegetable Lasagna

Caesar Salad

Chocolate Layer Cake

*2005 Tobacco Road Cabernet
Sauvignon "Vitality," Napa Valley*

Sunday Brunch with Friends

French Toast Strata with Cider Syrup

Mushroom Shallot Quiche

Cranberry Tart

Mushroom Shallot Quiche

1 (9-inch) refrigerator pie pastry
2¹/2 teaspoons chopped fresh thyme
1¹/2 tablespoons unsalted butter
¹/3 cup chopped shallots (about 2 medium)
8 ounces white mushrooms, trimmed and
    cut into ¹/4-inch slices
Salt and black pepper to taste
2¹/2 teaspoons chopped fresh thyme
1 cup (4 ounces) shredded Gruyère cheese
4 eggs
2 cups half-and-half
3/4 teaspoon salt
¹/4 teaspoon freshly ground black pepper
¹/8 teaspoon cayenne pepper

Fit the pastry into a 9-inch pie plate, crimping or fluting the edge in a decorative manner. Sprinkle 2¹/2 teaspoons thyme over the bottom of the pastry. Melt the butter in a large nonstick skillet over medium heat. Add the shallots and sauté for 2 minutes or until tender. Stir in the mushrooms and season with salt and black pepper to taste. Increase the heat to high.

Sauté for 8 minutes or until the liquid is absorbed and the mushrooms are tender. Sprinkle with 2¹/2 teaspoons thyme and sauté for 1 minute longer. Let stand until cool. Drain any remaining moisture from the mushrooms. Spread the mushrooms over the bottom of the pastry. Sprinkle with the cheese.

Lightly whisk the eggs in a bowl. Add the half-and-half, 3/4 teaspoon salt, ¹/4 teaspoon black pepper and the cayenne pepper and whisk until combined. Pour over the prepared layers. Bake in a preheated 425-degree oven for 15 minutes. Reduce the temperature to 300 degrees and bake for 30 minutes longer or until a knife inserted halfway into the center comes out clean. Let stand for 15 minutes before slicing.

A favorite menu item served at Faculty and Staff Appreciation Luncheons.

Serves 6 to 8

Country Ham Rolls

3/4 cup (1 1/2 sticks) butter, softened
3/4 cup packed light brown sugar
3 (12-count) packages frozen yeast rolls,
    slightly thawed
1 pound country ham or prosciutto,
    shaved or very thinly sliced

Mix the butter and brown sugar in a bowl until blended. Remove the rolls from the pans and slice each pan horizontally into halves to make one large roll; do not separate the rolls. Spread the butter mixture evenly over the cut sides of the layers. Top each bottom layer with one-third of the ham and the remaining top layers of the rolls. Return the prepared rolls to the foil pans.

Bake, covered with foil, in a preheated 350-degree oven for 20 to 30 minutes or until the rolls are brown and the filling is heated through. Remove from the pan and cut into individual rolls. Serve warm.

A favorite menu item served at Faculty and Staff Appreciation Luncheons.

Makes 3 dozen rolls

This recipe is a nice change from the traditional ham biscuit. The sweet-salty combination is addictive.

French Toast Strata with Cider Syrup

French Toast
1 (1-pound) loaf supermarket French bread,
    cut into chunks
8 ounces cream cheese, cut into cubes
8 eggs
2 1/2 cups milk
1/2 cup (1 stick) butter, melted
1/4 cup maple syrup

Cider Syrup
1/2 cup sugar
4 teaspoons cornstarch
1/2 teaspoon (or less) cinnamon
1 cup apple juice or apple cider
1 tablespoon lemon juice
2 teaspoons butter

To prepare the French toast, layer one-half of the bread in a greased 3-quart baking dish. Top with the cream cheese and the remaining bread. Whisk the eggs, milk, butter and maple syrup in a bowl until blended. Pour over the prepared layers and press lightly to help ensure the bread cubes are covered.

Chill, covered with plastic wrap, for 2 to 24 hours. Bake in a preheated 325-degree oven for 35 minutes. Increase the oven temperature to 350 degrees and bake for 15 minutes longer.

To prepare the syrup, combine the sugar, cornstarch and cinnamon in a saucepan and mix well. Stir in the apple juice. Bring to a boil and boil for 2 to 3 minutes, stirring occasionally. Stir in the lemon juice and butter and remove from the heat. Serve warm with the French toast. This recipe yields 1 1/3 cups of syrup. Double the recipe if needed.

Serves 8

Raving Recipes, the first Ravenscroft community cookbook, was published in 1995. *Excellent Courses* includes select recipes from this original cookbook, reprinted to preserve our legacy. The Ravenscroft formal crest adorns those pages.

Savory Southern Biscuits

1 1/2 cups cake flour
2 teaspoons garlic powder
2 teaspoons dried oregano
2 teaspoons dried thyme
2 teaspoons sugar
1 3/4 teaspoons baking powder
1 1/2 teaspoons paprika
1/4 teaspoon salt
3 tablespoons unsalted butter, chilled and
    cut into small pieces
3/4 cup heavy cream

Combine the cake flour, garlic powder, oregano, thyme, sugar, baking powder, paprika and salt in a food processor and pulse until combined. Add the butter and pulse until crumbly. Add the cream and process until the dough forms a ball.

Remove the dough from the food processor and knead on a lightly floured surface. Roll 1/4 inch thick. Cut into 1 1/2-inch rounds using a biscuit cutter or small jar. Arrange the rounds in a single layer on a baking sheet lined with baking parchment.

Bake in a preheated 400-degree oven for 10 to 15 minutes or until light brown.

Delicious stuffed with country ham or sausage.

Makes 1 dozen biscuits

Sweet Potato Angel Biscuits

2 sweet potatoes
1 envelope dry yeast
$^1/_4$ cup warm (105- to 115-degree) water
$2^1/_2$ cups all-purpose flour
$^1/_2$ cup sugar
1 teaspoon baking powder
1 teaspoon salt
$^1/_2$ cup shortening

Bake the sweet potatoes in a preheated 375-degree oven for 1 hour or until tender. Cool slightly and peel. Mash enough of the sweet potato pulp in a bowl to yield 1 cup. Reserve any remaining sweet potato pulp for another use. Cover to keep warm. Mix the yeast and warm water in a liquid measuring cup. Let stand for 5 minutes.

Mix the flour, sugar, baking powder and salt in a large bowl. Cut in the shortening with a pastry blender or fork until crumbly. Add the mashed sweet potatoes and yeast mixture and stir until moistened. Place the dough in a mixing bowl of a large stand mixer fitted with a dough hook and knead for 5 minutes. Or, knead on a lightly floured surface for 5 minutes. Place the dough in a lightly greased bowl, turning to coat the surface. Chill, covered, for 8 to 10 hours.

Roll the dough $^1/_2$ inch thick on a lightly floured surface. Cut into rounds with a 2-inch biscuit cutter; do not twist the cutter. Arrange the rounds in a single layer on an ungreased baking sheet. Let rise, covered, in a warm place (85 degrees) free from drafts for 20 minutes or until doubled in bulk. Bake on the middle oven rack in a preheated 400-degree oven for 10 to 12 minutes or until light brown. Serve warm.

Makes $2^1/_2$ dozen biscuits

Pumpkin Apple Streusel Muffins

Muffins
2 1/2 cups all-purpose flour
2 cups sugar
1 tablespoon pumpkin pie spice
1 1/2 teaspoons salt
1 teaspoon baking soda
1 cup canned solid pumpkin
1/2 cup vegetable oil
2 eggs, lightly beaten
2 cups finely chopped peeled apples

Streusel Topping
1/4 cup sugar
2 tablespoons all-purpose flour
1/2 teaspoon cinnamon
4 teaspoons butter

To prepare the muffins, mix the flour, sugar, pie spice, salt and baking soda in a large bowl. Combine the pumpkin, oil and eggs in a bowl and mix well. Add to the flour mixture and stir just until moistened. Fold in the apples. Fill greased or paper-lined muffin cups three-fourths full.

To prepare the topping, combine the sugar, flour and cinnamon in a bowl and mix well. Cut in the butter until crumbly. Sprinkle evenly over the muffin batter. Bake in a preheated 350-degree oven for 35 to 40 minutes or until light brown. Cool in the pan for 2 minutes and remove to a wire rack.

Makes 1 dozen muffins

Marinated Vegetable Platter

Lemon Pesto Dressing
1 cup extra-virgin olive oil
1/2 cup lemon juice
2 tablespoons pesto
1 teaspoon crushed garlic
Salt and pepper to taste

Vegetable Platter
1 or 2 (13-ounce) cans artichoke hearts, drained
1 (10-ounce) jar pimento-stuffed large
    green olives, drained
1 (6-ounce) jar pitted Kalamata olives, drained
1 or 2 red, orange or yellow bell peppers, sliced
1 large purple onion, sliced
1 cucumber, peeled, seeded and coarsely chopped
1 fennel bulb, sliced
2 cups cherry tomatoes, cut into halves
8 ounces soft mozzarella cheese, cut into chunks
8 ounces Asiago cheese, cut into chunks
1/2 to 1 cup sliced salami (optional)
4 to 8 ounces prosciutto, rolled and sliced (optional)
1/2 to 1 cup sun-dried tomatoes, drained (optional)
Arugula or other salad greens
1/4 to 1/2 cup (1 to 2 ounces) shaved
    Parmesan cheese

To prepare the dressing, whisk the olive oil, lemon juice, pesto and garlic in a bowl until combined. Season with salt and pepper.

To prepare the platter, combine the artichokes, olives, bell pepper, onion, cucumber, fennel, cherry tomatoes, mozzarella cheese and Asiago cheese in a bowl. Mix in the salami, prosciutto and sun-dried tomatoes. Add the dressing and toss until coated. Marinate, covered, in the refrigerator for 1 hour or longer.

Line a large serving platter with arugula. Scatter the vegetables over the greens and sprinkle with the Parmesan cheese. This recipe makes a large amount but keeps in the refrigerator for days. The longer the marinating time, the better the flavor.

Serves 12

Spicy Pimento Cheese

1/4 cup mayonnaise
2 tablespoons chili sauce
2 teaspoons Worcestershire sauce
2 teaspoons dry sherry
2 teaspoons chili powder
2 cups (8 ounces) shredded sharp Cheddar cheese
1/2 cup finely chopped drained jarred roasted
    red peppers
1/4 cup finely chopped red onion
Salt to taste

Combine the mayonnaise, chili sauce, Worcestershire sauce, sherry and chili powder in a bowl and mix well. Stir in the cheese, peppers and onion. Season with salt.

Chill, covered, for 1 hour or longer. Spread on your favorite variety of bread or crackers.

Makes 2 cups

Crostini sounds fancy, but it's just an Italian term for toppings on toasted bread. Try spreading local herbed goat cheese on thin baguette slices. Broil until melted and toasty. Top with pepper relish. Quick, easy, and delicious.

Savory Chicken Crescents

3 ounces cream cheese, softened
2 tablespoons butter, melted
2 cups chopped cooked chicken
2 tablespoons milk
1 tablespoon chopped chives
1/4 teaspoon salt
1/8 teaspoon pepper
2 (8-count) cans crescent rolls

Mix the cream cheese and butter in a bowl until blended. Stir in the chicken, milk, chives, salt and pepper.

Unroll the crescent roll dough and separate into sixteen triangles. Spoon 1 heaping tablespoon of the chicken mixture in the center of each triangle. Fold the triangles point to point and crimp the edges with a fork. Arrange the crescents on an ungreased baking sheet. Bake in a preheated 350-degree oven for 12 to 18 minutes or until golden brown.

Makes 16

*G*ive plain cream cheese an Asian flair for a quick and easy appetizer. Pour tamari over the top and sprinkle with sesame seeds. Serve with rice crackers.

Empanadas

8 ounces boneless skinless chicken thighs,
    cut into $1/2$-inch pieces
$1/4$ cup minced onion
$1/2$ green bell pepper, minced
4 pimento-stuffed green olives, coarsely chopped
2 tablespoons golden raisins
2 tablespoons chicken broth
2 tablespoons tomato paste
1 tablespoon chopped fresh parsley
1 teaspoon ground cumin
1 garlic clove, minced
$1/2$ teaspoon salt
$1/2$ teaspoon freshly ground pepper
36 won ton wrappers
Salt to taste

Combine the chicken, onion, bell pepper, olives, raisins, broth, tomato paste, parsley, cumin, garlic, $1/2$ teaspoon salt and the pepper in a large nonstick skillet. Cook over medium heat until the chicken is cooked through, stirring frequently. Process the chicken mixture in a food processor until coarsely chopped. Chill, covered, for 30 minutes.

Arrange one won ton wrapper on a hard work surface and lightly brush the edges with water. Place 1 heaping teaspoon of the chicken mixture in the center of the wrapper and fold over to enclose the filling. Press the edges with a fork to seal. Arrange the empanada on a baking sheet lightly coated with nonstick cooking spray. Repeat the process with the remaining won ton wrappers and the remaining chicken mixture. Lightly spray the empanadas with nonstick cooking spray and sprinkle with salt to taste.

Bake in a preheated 400-degree oven for 10 to 12 minutes or until golden brown, turning halfway through the baking process.

A favorite snack of Upper School Spanish students for Cinco de Mayo.

Makes 3 dozen empanadas

Sausage-Stuffed Mushrooms

24 ounces white button mushrooms
1 pound sweet Italian sausage, casings removed
2 shallots, minced
4 garlic cloves, minced
Salt and pepper to taste
1 to 2 tablespoons olive oil
1/4 cup parsley, minced
1 cup herb-seasoned stuffing mix or fresh
    bread crumbs
1/4 cup (1 ounce) grated Parmesan cheese
1 egg, beaten

Remove the stems from the mushrooms and finely chop; reserve the mushroom caps. Brown the sausage in a skillet, stirring until crumbly. Remove the sausage to a bowl using a slotted spoon, reserving the pan drippings.

Sauté the mushroom stems, shallots, garlic, salt and pepper in the reserved pan drippings until the mushrooms are tender, adding the olive oil as needed to keep the mushrooms moist. Stir in the parsley and remove from the heat.

Add the sausage, stuffing mix and cheese to the mushroom mixture and mix well. Season with salt and pepper and stir in the egg. Mound in the mushroom caps and arrange the mushrooms in a single layer on a baking sheet. Bake in a preheated 350-degree oven for 20 to 30 minutes or until heated through.

Makes 2 to 3 dozen mushrooms

Scallops in Champagne Saffron Sauce

1/4 cup (1/2 stick) butter
2 1/4 pounds bay scallops
1 1/2 cups Champagne
Pinch of saffron
1 cup whipping cream
1 teaspoon lemon juice
1/4 teaspoon salt
1/4 teaspoon pepper

Melt the butter in a large skillet and add the scallops. Cook over medium heat for 3 minutes or until the scallops are tender, stirring constantly. Drain, discarding the pan drippings. Remove the scallops to a bowl.

Combine the Champagne and saffron in the same skillet and bring to a boil over medium heat. Cook for 7 minutes or until the mixture is reduced by half. Stir in the cream, lemon juice, salt and pepper. Cook for 10 minutes or until thickened. Return the scallops to the skillet and cook over low heat just until heated through.

Serves 10 to 12

Beef and Sausage Chili

2 pounds bulk pork sausage
2 pounds ground beef
2 large yellow onions, chopped
2 (28-ounce) cans crushed tomatoes
2 (28-ounce) cans whole tomatoes,
    coarsely chopped
2 (10-ounce) can tomatoes with green chiles
2 (15-ounce) cans tomato sauce
2 (12-ounce) cans light beer
1/2 cup chili powder
1/4 cup ground cumin
4 garlic cloves, chopped
2 teaspoons oregano
2 teaspoons cayenne pepper

Brown the sausage and ground beef in a heavy stockpot, stirring until crumbly. Drain some of the pan drippings and then stir in the onions, tomatoes, tomato sauce and beer. Add the chili powder, cumin, garlic, oregano and cayenne pepper and mix well.

Simmer over low heat for 1 hour, stirring occasionally and adding water if needed for a thinner consistency. Ladle into chili bowls.

A favorite menu item served at Faculty and Staff Appreciation Luncheons.

Serves 24

*T*his is a great hearty chili for a crowd. The recipe can easily be halved.

Vegetarian Bean Chili

2 tablespoons vegetable oil
2 onions, finely chopped
1 red bell pepper, chopped
1/4 cup medium-hot chili powder
1 tablespoon ground cumin
6 garlic cloves, minced
3 (14-ounce) cans diced tomatoes
1 cup water
1/2 teaspoon salt
1 (15-ounce) can red kidney beans,
    drained and rinsed
2 (15-ounce) cans pinto beans, drained and rinsed
1 (15-ounce) can black beans, drained and rinsed
1/2 cup chopped fresh cilantro
Salt and pepper to taste

Heat the oil in a large Dutch oven over medium heat until shimmering. Stir in the onions, bell pepper, chili powder and cumin. Cook for 7 minutes or until the onions are tender. Stir in the garlic and cook for 15 seconds. Stir in the tomatoes, water and 1/2 teaspoon salt and bring to a simmer.

Simmer, covered, for 30 minutes, stirring occasionally. Add the beans and simmer, uncovered, for 30 minutes longer or until the chili is slightly thickened. Stir in the cilantro and season with salt and pepper to taste. Ladle into chili bowls.

A favorite menu item served at Faculty and Staff Luncheons.

Serves 6 to 8

This chili is nice and hearty. You will not even miss the meat. Great served over brown rice.

Tailgate Corn Chowder

1/4 cup olive oil
1/4 cup (1/2 stick) butter
2 cups chopped yellow onions
1 cup chopped celery
1/2 cup all-purpose flour
2 teaspoons kosher salt
1 teaspoon pepper
12 cups vegetable broth
6 cups coarsely chopped Yukon gold potatoes
10 cups frozen corn kernels (about 3 pounds)
2 cups shredded carrots
2 cups half-and-half
8 ounces sharp white Cheddar cheese, shredded
Kosher salt and pepper to taste

Heat the olive oil and butter in a large stockpot over medium heat until the butter melts. Stir in the onions and celery and cook for 10 minutes or until the vegetables are tender. Add the flour, 2 teaspoons salt and 1 teaspoon pepper and mix well.

Cook for 3 minutes, stirring frequently. Stir in the broth and potatoes and bring to a boil. Reduce the heat to low and simmer for 15 minutes or until the potatoes are tender. Add the corn and carrots and mix well. Stir in the half-and-half and cheese and cook for 5 minutes longer. Season with salt and pepper to taste and ladle into soup bowls.

A favorite menu item served at Faculty and Staff Appreciation Luncheons.

Serves 10 to 12

Baked Onion Soup

3 tablespoons butter
1 tablespoon extra-virgin olive oil
6 cups thinly sliced yellow onions
1 teaspoon salt
1/2 teaspoon sugar
2 tablespoons all-purpose flour
2 quarts (8 cups) organic beef
    stock, heated
2 cups French triple-dry vermouth
1 1/2 cups heavy cream
2 tablespoons Kitchen Bouquet
Salt and freshly ground pepper to taste

2 baguettes French bread, cut into
    1/2-inch slices
Butter for coating
8 ounces Emmentaler cheese,
    finely sliced
1/4 cup Cognac (optional)
4 ounces Swiss Gruyère cheese,
    coarsely grated
1/2 cup (2 ounces) freshly grated
    Parmesan cheese
2 tablespoons butter

Heat 3 tablespoons butter and the olive oil in a heavy 4-quart stockpot. Add the onions and cook, covered, over medium-low heat for 15 to 20 minutes or until the onions are tender. Increase the heat to medium-high and stir in 1 teaspoon salt and the sugar. Cook for 20 to 30 minutes longer or until the onions are caramelized and reduced to 1 cup, stirring frequently. Watch carefully to avoid burning the onions.

Decrease the heat to medium and stir in the flour. Cook for 2 to 3 minutes, stirring constantly. Remove from the heat and stir in 1 cup of the stock. Add the remaining stock, the vermouth, cream and Kitchen Bouquet and mix well. Season lightly with salt and pepper to taste. Return to the stovetop and bring to a boil. Reduce the heat and simmer, partially covered, for 30 minutes. Arrange the baguette slices in a single layer on a baking sheet. Toast in a preheated 425-degree oven until brown. Watch carefully. Remove the bread from the oven and decrease the temperature to 350 degrees.

Coat the bottom of individual ovenproof soup tureens, ovenproof ramekins or a large ovenproof tureen with butter. Layer with some of the toasted baguette slices, some of the Emmentaler cheese and sprinkle with pepper. Top with another layer of toasted baguette slices and Emmentaler cheese. Ladle the boiling soup over the prepared layers and drizzle evenly with the brandy. Float a layer of the toasted baguette slices over the top and sprinkle with Gruyère cheese. Sprinkle with pepper and Parmesan cheese. Dot evenly with 2 tablespoons butter. Arrange the tureens on a baking sheet on the middle oven rack. Bake for 30 minutes or until light brown and bubbly. Broil until brown. Serve immediately to avoid the baguette slices from sinking.

Serves 6 to 8

This soup is so hearty—just add a big salad for a complete meal.

Sausage Tortellini Soup

1 pound mild ground Italian sausage
1 large onion, chopped
1 garlic clove, crushed
3 (14-ounce) cans beef broth
2 (14-ounce) cans diced tomatoes
1 1/2 cups dry red wine
1 (8-ounce) can tomato sauce
2 carrots, thinly sliced
1 tablespoon sugar
2 teaspoons Italian seasoning
2 small zucchini, sliced
1 (14-ounce) package refrigerator cheese tortellini
1 cup (4 ounces) shredded Parmesan cheese

Brown the sausage with the onion and garlic in a Dutch oven over medium heat, stirring until the sausage is crumbly and no longer pink and the onion is tender; drain on paper towels. Return the sausage mixture to the Dutch oven and stir in the broth, tomatoes, wine, tomato sauce, carrots, sugar and Italian seasoning.

Bring to a boil and then reduce the heat. Simmer for 30 minutes. Skim off any fat and stir in the zucchini, pasta and cheese. Simmer for 10 minutes longer. Ladle into soup bowls.

Serves 10

Napa Cabbage Salad

Soy Dressing
1/2 cup vegetable oil
1/2 cup soy sauce
1/4 cup sugar
1/4 cup white vinegar or rice vinegar

Salad
8 cups shredded Napa cabbage (1 large head)
1 package broccoli slaw
1 cup shredded carrots
1 cup thinly sliced green onions
2 tablespoons butter
1/2 cup slivered almonds
2 (3-ounce) packages ramen noodles, broken

To prepare the dressing, combine the oil, soy sauce, sugar and vinegar in a jar with a tight-fitting lid and seal tightly. Shake to combine.

To prepare the salad, toss the cabbage, slaw, carrots and green onions in a large bowl. Melt the butter in a large nonstick skillet and add the almonds and noodles. Cook over medium-low heat for 5 to 10 minutes or until light brown, stirring occasionally. Remove to a plate to cool.

Just before serving, add the almond mixture to the salad and mix well. Add the dressing and toss to coat. Serve immediately.

A favorite menu item served at Faculty and Staff Appreciation Luncheons.

Serves 8 to 10

Caesar Salad

Creamy Anchovy Dressing
1/2 cup mayonnaise
2 teaspoons Worcestershire sauce
Juice of 1 lemon
3 garlic cloves, minced
1 1/2 teaspoons anchovy paste
1 teaspoon coarsely ground pepper
1/4 teaspoon salt

Salad
2 heads romaine, torn
1 cup (4 ounces) shredded Parmesan cheese
1 cup croutons
1/2 pint grape tomatoes, cut into halves
1/2 cup pine nuts, toasted

To prepare the dressing, combine the mayonnaise, Worcestershire sauce, lemon juice, garlic, anchovy paste, pepper and salt in a bowl and whisk until combined. Store, covered, in the refrigerator for up to 1 week.

To prepare the salad, toss the romaine, cheese and croutons in a large bowl. Add just enough of the dressing to lightly coat and mix well. Sprinkle with the tomatoes and pine nuts and toss again.

Thinly sliced pepperoni cut into slivers makes a nice addition to the salad. A favorite menu item served at Faculty and Staff Appreciation Luncheons.

Serves 8

Spinach, Apple and Bacon Salad

Dijon Vinaigrette

1/4 cup olive oil
2 tablespoons white wine vinegar
2 teaspoons Dijon mustard
1 teaspoon soy sauce
1/2 teaspoon curry powder
1/2 teaspoon sugar

Salad

12 ounces spinach, stems removed
1 cup chopped green apple
6 slices bacon, crisp-cooked and crumbled
1/4 cup pine nuts, toasted

To prepare the vinaigrette, combine the olive oil, vinegar, Dijon mustard, soy sauce, curry powder and sugar in a jar with a tight-fitting lid and seal tightly. Shake to mix.

To prepare the salad, pour the vinaigrette in a serving bowl. Layer with the spinach, apple and bacon; do not toss. Chill, covered, in the refrigerator. Toss the salad and sprinkle with the pine nuts just before serving.

If you prefer a sweeter flavor, substitute your favorite red apple for the green apple.

Serves 6

Roasted Chicken Salad

2 or 3 small green onions
1 deli rotisserie chicken, skinned
2/3 cup (or more) mayonnaise
1 tablespoon fresh lemon juice
1 teaspoon chopped fresh tarragon
Salt and pepper to taste

Cut the white bulb and the light green part of the green onions into 1-inch pieces and place in the bowl of a food processor. Pulse a few times until finely chopped. Remove the meat from the chicken, discarding the bones. Add the chicken to the onion and process until finely chopped.

Combine the chicken mixture, mayonnaise, lemon juice and tarragon in a bowl and mix well, adding additional mayonnaise if needed for the desired consistency. Season with salt and pepper. Store, covered, in the refrigerator until serving time.

The chicken salad tastes best after being chilled for several hours. Serve alone, in a sandwich or with crackers.

Serves 4

Chicken Salad with Blue Cheese and Dried Cherries

2 tablespoons olive oil
1 1/2 to 2 pounds boneless skinless chicken breasts,
    cut into 1-inch pieces
1 teaspoon salt
1/2 teaspoon pepper
1 cup dried cherries
1/2 cup chopped celery
1/2 cup chopped walnuts, toasted
1/2 cup Roquefort cheese
1/2 cup blue cheese salad dressing

Heat the olive oil in a skillet over high heat. Add the chicken, salt and pepper. Cook for
5 minutes or until the chicken is cooked through and brown on all sides, stirring frequently.
Remove to a plate to cool.

Combine the chicken, cherries, celery and walnuts in a bowl and mix well. Add the cheese
and dressing and mix until coated. Chill, covered, for 1 hour.

Great served on fresh arugula or in a sandwich or wrap.

Serves 6

Mediterranean Pasta Salad

16 ounces tricolor rotini
2 cups broccoli florets, blanched and chopped
2 tomatoes, seeded and chopped
1 (8-ounce) jar marinated artichoke hearts,
    drained and chopped
3 carrots, shredded
1/2 cup drained sun-dried tomatoes, cut into slivers
1/2 cup (or more) crumbled feta cheese
1/4 cup sliced pitted Kalamata olives (optional)
3 tablespoons chopped fresh basil
1 cup balsamic vinaigrette
Salt and pepper to taste

Cook the pasta using the package directions. Drain and rinse with cold water; drain again. Combine the pasta, broccoli, fresh tomatoes, artichokes, carrots, sun-dried tomatoes, cheese, olives and basil in a bowl and mix well. Add the vinaigrette and toss until coated. Season with salt and pepper. Chill, covered, until serving time.

Serves 6 to 8

*A*dding grilled chicken breast strips or grilled shrimp would make a great lunch or warm weather supper.

Flank Steak in Wine Sauce

1 1/2 to 2 pounds flank steak
2/3 cup sherry
1 tablespoon soy sauce
2 1/2 cups sliced mushrooms
3 tablespoons chopped onion
2 1/2 tablespoons butter
1 small garlic clove, crushed
1 tablespoon cornstarch
1 (10-ounce) can beef broth
1 tablespoon ketchup
1 tablespoon mustard

Place the steak in a glass dish and pierce the surface with a fork. Pour the wine and soy sauce over the steak. Marinate, covered, in the refrigerator for 2 to 10 hours, turning occasionally. Drain, reserving 1/2 cup of the marinade. Grill or broil the steak 3 to 4 minutes per side for medium-rare. Remove to a platter.

Sauté the mushrooms and onion in the butter in a skillet. Add the garlic and reserved 1/2 cup marinade and mix well. Simmer for 5 minutes. Whisk the cornstarch and broth in a bowl until blended and add to the mushroom mixture. Stir in the ketchup and mustard and bring to a boil.

Boil until thickened and of a sauce consistency, stirring occasionally. Diagonally slice the steak into 1/4-inch strips and arrange on a serving platter. Pour the warm wine sauce over the steak and serve immediately.

Serves 4 to 6

Winston's Grille Meat Loaf

Meat Loaf
4 pounds ground beef
1 cup plus 2 tablespoons packed
  brown sugar
1 cup Italian-seasoned bread crumbs
1/2 cup finely chopped green bell pepper
1/2 cup finely chopped yellow onion
2/3 cup Heinz 57 Steak Sauce
2/3 cup ketchup
2 eggs, beaten
2 tablespoons Worcestershire sauce
2 tablespoons minced garlic
1 tablespoon salt
1 teaspoon white pepper

Brown Sugar Glaze
1/2 cup Worcestershire sauce
1/2 cup plus 1 tablespoon packed
  brown sugar
1/3 cup Heinz 57 Steak Sauce

Tomato Sauce
1 (14-ounce) can diced tomatoes
2 cups demi-glace
2/3 cup Heinz 57 Steak Sauce
1/2 teaspoon white pepper

To prepare the meat loaf, mix the ground beef, brown sugar, bread crumbs, bell pepper and onion in a bowl. Mix in the steak sauce, ketchup, eggs, Worcestershire sauce, garlic, salt and white pepper by hand. At this point the beef mixture may be stored, covered, in the refrigerator for 8 to 10 hours. Shape into a 2×7×10-inch loaf and place in a large broiler pan. Spray the top with nonstick cooking spray or rub lightly with vegetable oil. Cover the top of the loaf with baking parchment and then cover the entire pan with foil. Bake in a preheated 375-degree oven for 2 hours. Discard the foil and baking parchment.

To prepare the glaze, whisk the Worcestershire sauce, brown sugar and steak sauce in a bowl. Spread the glaze over the meatloaf and bake for 10 minutes longer.

To prepare the sauce, combine the tomatoes, demi-glace, steak sauce and white pepper in a saucepan and mix well. Bring to a boil and reduce the heat. Simmer for 5 minutes. Slice the meat loaf as desired and top each serving with some of the sauce.

For the demi-glace, use a demi-glace mix or brown gravy mix and prepare using the package directions, or prepare your own. It is much easier to purchase at your local supermarket. Winston's Grille prepares its own demi-glace from scratch using veal stock. They have been serving this meat loaf for over twenty years. If you want just one or two servings, they make it every Tuesday.

Serves 8 to 12

Winston's Grille is an upbeat eating establishment offering a creative menu of delicious food. The generosity of sharing this recipe mirrors the Winston family's long standing support of Ravenscroft.

Gingered Pork Tenderloins

2 pork tenderloins
1 orange
1/4 cup soy sauce
1/4 cup water
Juice of 1 lime
1 teaspoon grated fresh ginger
3 garlic cloves, crushed
1 red onion, thinly sliced

Arrange the tenderloins in a baking dish. Juice the orange into a bowl and then slice. Add the soy sauce, water, lime juice, ginger and garlic to the orange juice and mix well. Pour over the tenderloins, turning to coat.

Arrange the orange slices and onion over the pork. Bake in a preheated 350- to 400-degree oven for 20 to 30 minutes or until a meat thermometer registers 160 degrees for medium.

Serves 6 to 8

Tuscan Grilled Pork

12 garlic cloves
2 tablespoons olive oil
2 teaspoons fresh rosemary
1 teaspoon salt, or to taste
1 teaspoon coarsely ground pepper, or to taste
1/4 teaspoon dry mustard
1 (14- to 16-ounce) pork tenderloin

Combine the garlic, olive oil, rosemary, salt, pepper and dry mustard in a food processor or blender. Pulse until of a paste consistency. Rub the surface of the tenderloin with the garlic paste.

Grill the tenderloin over hot coals until a meat thermometer registers 160 degrees for medium. Let rest for 5 to 10 minutes before slicing.

The garlic paste is also good on thick-cut pork chops or veal chops and butterflied leg of lamb.

Serves 4

Sausage-Stuffed Acorn Squash

2 acorn squash
12 to 16 ounces low-fat bulk pork sausage
1 1/2 cups chopped Granny Smith apples
1 1/2 cups (6 ounces) shredded Cheddar cheese
1/2 cup dry plain bread crumbs
Salt and pepper to taste

Stand the squash on end and cut into halves. Discard the seeds and membranes. Arrange the squash cut side down in a microwave-safe dish. Microwave for 10 to 12 minutes or until the squash is easily pierced with a fork. Or, bake in a preheated 350-degree oven for about 30 minutes or until tender.

Brown the sausage in a skillet, stirring until crumbly; drain. Add the apples and cook until the apples are tender. Stir in the cheese and bread crumbs.

Arrange the squash cut side up in a baking pan and sprinkle with salt and pepper. Fill the squash cavities equally with the sausage mixture. Bake in a preheated 350-degree oven for 20 to 30 minutes or until brown. Serve the squash halves either scooped out or in the shells with hot cooked rice on the side. You may substitute 1 1/2 cups tart applesauce for the Granny Smith apples.

Add a tossed salad for a complete meal.

Serves 4

Greek Chicken Breasts

^{1}/4 cup all-purpose flour
1 tablespoon oregano
Salt and pepper to taste
4 boneless skinless chicken breasts
3 tablespoons olive oil
^{1}/3 cup dry white wine
^{1}/3 cup chicken broth
2 ripe tomatoes, peeled and chopped
3 tablespoons sliced kalamata olives or black olives
2 tablespoons capers, drained
2 tablespoons crumbled feta cheese

Mix the flour, oregano, salt and pepper in a shallow dish. Coat the chicken in the flour mixture. Heat the olive oil in a large skillet over medium heat. Add the chicken and cook for 10 minutes, turning once. Add the wine and broth.

Simmer for 10 to 15 minutes, stirring occasionally. Stir in the tomatoes, olives and capers. Cook until heated through. Arrange the chicken on a serving platter and spoon the tomato mixture over the chicken. Sprinkle with the cheese and serve immediately. You may substitute one cup canned diced tomatoes for the fresh tomatoes.

Serves 4

Spicy Oven-Fried Chicken

1 1/4 cups buttermilk
1/4 cup extra-virgin olive oil
3 tablespoons hot pepper sauce
2 tablespoons Dijon mustard
2 garlic cloves, minced
1 teaspoon salt
1/2 teaspoon black pepper
1 large onion, sliced
12 chicken pieces with skin and bones
    (breasts, thighs and/or legs)
1 cup dry unseasoned bread crumbs
1/3 cup freshly grated Parmesan cheese
1/4 cup all-purpose flour
2 teaspoons dried thyme
1 teaspoon salt
1/2 teaspoon paprika
1/2 teaspoon cayenne pepper
3 tablespoons butter, melted

Whisk the buttermilk, olive oil, hot sauce, Dijon mustard, garlic, 1 teaspoon salt and the black pepper in a large bowl until combined. Add the onion and chicken and turn to coat. Marinate, covered, in the refrigerator for 3 to 24 hours, turning the chicken occasionally.

Arrange two baking racks on two large rimmed baking sheets. Whisk the bread crumbs, cheese, flour, thyme, 1 teaspoon salt, the paprika and cayenne pepper in a large shallow dish. Remove the chicken from the marinade, allowing any excess marinade to drip off. Coat the chicken with the bread crumb mixture and arrange skin side up on the baking racks. Let stand for 30 minutes.

Drizzle the butter over the chicken. Bake in a preheated 425-degree oven for 50 minutes or until the chicken is cooked through, golden brown and crisp. Serve warm or at room temperature.

Serves 6

Spanish Fish

1 large onion, chopped
2 tablespoons olive oil
1 (28-ounce) can crushed tomatoes
3 ounces pimento-stuffed green olives, sliced
2 tablespoons capers
2 teaspoons chili powder
1 teaspoon salt
1 teaspoon oregano
$^1/_2$ teaspoon pepper
4 to 6 fish fillets such as tilapia or Spanish mackerel

Sauté the onion in the olive oil in a saucepan until the onion is tender. Add the tomatoes and simmer for 5 minutes. Stir in the olives, capers, chili powder, salt, oregano and pepper.

Arrange the fillets in a single layer in a baking pan lined with foil. Spoon the tomato sauce over the fillets. Bake in a preheated 350-degree oven for 30 minutes, basting occasionally with the sauce.

Serves 4 to 6

Baked Seafood Salad

1 small onion, chopped
1 cup chopped celery
1 large green bell pepper, chopped (optional)
1 tablespoon butter
1 cup cooked lump crab meat
1 cup cooked shrimp, cut into bite-size pieces
1 cup cooked lobster meat, cut into bite-size pieces
1/2 cup mayonnaise
1 teaspoon Worcestershire sauce
1/4 teaspoon salt
1/8 teaspoon black pepper
Old Bay seasoning or cayenne pepper to taste
1 tablespoon butter
1/4 cup bread crumbs

Sauté the onion, celery and bell pepper in 1 tablespoon butter in a skillet until the onion is tender. Remove the onion mixture to a large bowl and stir in the crab meat, shrimp and lobster meat.

Combine the mayonnaise, Worcestershire sauce, salt, black pepper and Old Bay seasoning in a small bowl and mix well. Add to the crab meat mixture and mix gently.

Melt 1 tablespoon butter in a small skillet and add the bread crumbs. Cook for 1 minute or until brown, stirring constantly. Divide the seafood salad evenly among six ramekins and sprinkle with the bread crumbs. Bake in a preheated 300-degree oven for 30 minutes.

Serves 6

The late Reverend Bruce "Daniel" Sapp, Rector of Christ Church for thirty-six years and Chaplain of Ravenscroft School from 1957 to 1966, was instrumental in the founding of Wake Relief, a food bank still operated by Christ Church. Enjoy his Baked Seafood Salad, lovingly submitted by his family.

Easy Shrimp Pasta

1/2 cup balsamic vinaigrette
1 pound shrimp, peeled and deveined
2 cups chopped fresh tomatoes (about 4)
1/4 cup fresh basil leaves, chopped
4 ounces cream cheese, cut into cubes
12 ounces fettuccini, cooked and drained
1/4 cup fresh basil leaves, chopped
1 cup (4 ounces) shredded Italian cheese blend

Pour the vinaigrette over the shrimp in a shallow dish, turning to coat. Marinate in the refrigerator for 20 minutes. Drain, discarding the marinade.

Heat a large skillet over medium heat. Spoon in the shrimp and cook for 3 minutes or until the shrimp turn pink, stirring frequently. Remove to a bowl using a slotted spoon. Cover to keep warm.

Combine the tomatoes and 1/4 cup basil in the same skillet. Cook for 3 minutes, stirring constantly. Add the cream cheese and cook until combined. Add the shrimp and cook just until heated through, stirring occasionally. Spoon the hot pasta on a large serving platter. Top with the shrimp sauce and sprinkle with 1/4 cup basil and the Italian cheese blend. Serve immediately.

Serves 4 to 6

Italian Vegetable Lasagna

16 ounces lasagna noodles
Salt to taste
3 tablespoons olive oil
1 small to medium eggplant, chopped
1 cup chopped onion
1 cup sliced white mushrooms
4 ripe Roma tomatoes, chopped
1 small zucchini, thinly sliced
1 tablespoon chopped fresh basil
1/2 teaspoon salt
1/4 teaspoon pepper
2 cups (8 ounces) shredded mozzarella cheese
2 cups ricotta cheese
1/2 cup (2 ounces) grated Parmesan cheese
2 eggs, lightly beaten
1 cup marinara sauce
1/2 cup (2 ounces) shredded mozzarella cheese

Cook the pasta in boiling salted water in a saucepan using the package directions until
al dente. Drain and rinse. Heat the olive oil in a large skillet over medium-high heat and
add the eggplant, onion and mushrooms. Sauté for 10 to15 minutes or until the vegetables
are tender. Stir in the tomatoes, zucchini, basil, 1/2 teaspoon salt and the pepper. Reduce
the heat to medium and cook, covered, for 10 to 15 minutes or to the desired consistency,
stirring occasionally. Remove from the heat. Combine 2 cups mozzarella cheese, the
ricotta cheese, Parmesan cheese and eggs in a bowl and mix well.

Spread 1/2 cup of the marinara sauce in the bottom of a 9×13-inch baking dish sprayed
with nonstick cooking spray. Layer with a single layer of the pasta, one-half of the ricotta
cheese mixture and one-half of the sautéed vegetables. Top with a single layer of the
remaining pasta, the remaining ricotta cheese mixture and the remaining sautéed vegetables.
Layer with a single layer of the remaining pasta, the remaining 1/2 cup marinara sauce and
1/2 cup mozzarella cheese. Bake, covered with nonstick foil, in a preheated 375-degree
oven for 35 to 40 minutes. Remove the foil and bake for 10 to 15 minutes longer or
until brown.

Serves 6 to 8

Garlic Broccoli

1 1/2 pounds fresh broccoli, trimmed and cut into spears
1 1/2 teaspoons dark sesame oil
1 1/2 teaspoons vegetable oil
1/2 teaspoon crushed dried red pepper
2 garlic cloves, minced
1/4 cup soy sauce
1 tablespoon sugar
1 tablespoon lemon juice
1 tablespoon water

Steam the broccoli for 5 minutes or until tender-crisp. Remove from heat and keep warm. Heat the sesame oil and vegetable oil in a small saucepan until hot but not smoking. Remove from the heat.

Stir the red pepper into the sesame oil mixture and let stand for 10 minutes. Add the garlic, soy sauce, sugar, lemon juice and water and stir until the sugar dissolves. Toss the broccoli with the sesame oil mixture in a bowl. Serve warm or chilled.

Serves 4

Rosemary Spoon Bread

2 1/2 tablespoons butter
1 cup water-ground yellow cornmeal
1 teaspoon salt
1 cup boiling water
1 cup whole or 2% milk
1 egg, lightly beaten
2 tablespoons fresh rosemary

Melt the butter in a 1-quart baking dish in a preheated 450-degree oven. Maintain the oven temperature.

Sift the cornmeal and salt into a heatproof bowl and mix well. Stir in the boiling water. Add the milk and egg and mix well. Stir in the rosemary. Pour into the prepared baking dish. Bake for 35 to 45 minutes or until light golden brown. Serve warm.

Serves 4

Wild Mushroom Bread Pudding

1 loaf French bread, cut into chunks
1/4 cup olive oil
4 teaspoons chopped fresh thyme
1 large garlic clove, minced
Salt and pepper to taste
6 tablespoons butter
2 pounds assorted fresh mushrooms, such as cremini,
    button, portobello and shiitake, thinly sliced
1/2 cup finely chopped shallots
1/2 cup chopped fresh parsley
3 1/2 cups heavy whipping cream
8 eggs
2 teaspoons salt
1 teaspoon freshly ground pepper
1/2 cup (2 ounces) grated Parmesan cheese

Toss the bread, olive oil, thyme and garlic in a bowl to coat. Spread the bread in a single layer on a large rimmed baking sheet. Season with salt and pepper to taste. Toast in a preheated 350-degree oven for 20 minutes or until golden brown and slightly crunchy, stirring occasionally. Return the toasted bread to the same bowl.

Melt 6 tablespoons butter in a large skillet over medium-high heat. Add the mushrooms and shallots and season with salt and pepper to taste. Sauté for 15 minutes or until the mushrooms are tender and the juices have evaporated. Stir in the parsley. Add the mushroom mixture to the bread and toss to combine.

Spread in a buttered 9x13-inch baking dish. Whisk the cream, eggs, 2 teaspoons salt and 1 teaspoon pepper in a large bowl until blended. Pour over the prepared layer and sprinkle with the cheese. Bake in a preheated 350-degree oven for 1 hour or until the custard is set and the top is golden brown.

Serves 8 to 10

Kale with Roasted Red Peppers and Olives

2 large bunches kale
2 tablespoons olive oil
2 garlic cloves, thinly sliced
1/4 cup water
12 kalamata olives, pitted and chopped
1 (4-ounce) jar roasted red peppers, drained
2 teaspoons sugar
1 teaspoon salt
2 tablespoons aged balsamic vinegar

Trim the kale and tear into bite-size pieces. Rinse and pat dry. Heat the olive oil and garlic in a large skillet over medium-high heat. Add the kale and stir-fry for 5 minutes. Stir in the water.

Cook, covered, for 10 minutes. Stir in the olives, roasted red peppers, sugar and salt. Cook over medium heat until heated through. Spoon into a serving bowl and drizzle with the vinegar.

Serves 4 to 6

Fall signals the start of the root vegetable season. Try tossing chunks of butternut squash with a little olive oil and honey. Season with salt and pepper and roast until tender.

Chocolate Layer Cake

Butter for coating
All-purpose flour for dusting
1 3/4 cups all-purpose flour
1 cup good-quality baking cocoa
1 1/2 teaspoons baking soda
1/4 teaspoon salt
3/4 cup (1 1/2 sticks) unsalted butter, softened
2/3 cup granulated sugar
2/3 cup packed light brown sugar
2 eggs, at room temperature
2 teaspoons vanilla extract
1 cup buttermilk, at room temperature
1/2 cup sour cream, at room temperature

Coat two 8-inch cake pans with butter. Line the bottoms with waxed paper and coat the waxed paper with butter. Dust the pans with flour, shaking out any excess.

Sift 1 3/4 cups flour, the baking cocoa, baking soda and salt together. Cream 3/4 cup butter, the granulated sugar and brown sugar in a mixing bowl for 5 minutes. Add the eggs and vanilla and beat until blended. Mix the buttermilk and sour cream in a small bowl.

With the mixer on low speed, add the buttermilk mixture and dry ingredients alternately to the creamed mixture, beating just until combined after each addition and ending with the dry ingredients. Spoon the batter evenly into the prepared pans.

Bake in a preheated 350-degree oven for 25 to 30 minutes or until wooden picks inserted in the centers come out clean. Cool in the pans on a wire rack for 10 minutes. Remove the layers to the wire rack and let stand until completely cool. Frost with your favorite frosting.

Serves 10

Pumpkin Pound Cake with Brown Sugar Glaze

Pumpkin Cake
3 cups all-purpose flour
2 teaspoons baking powder
2 teaspoons cinnamon
1/2 teaspoon baking soda
1/2 teaspoon salt
1/4 teaspoon ground cloves
1/8 teaspoon apple pie spice
2 cups canned pumpkin
1/3 cup rum

1 cup (2 sticks) butter, softened
3 cups sugar
5 eggs

Brown Sugar Glaze
3 tablespoons butter
3 tablespoons light brown sugar
3 tablespoons granulated sugar
3 tablespoons heavy whipping cream
1/2 teaspoon vanilla extract

To prepare the cake, mix the flour, baking powder, cinnamon, baking soda, salt, cloves and apple pie spice in a bowl. Combine the pumpkin and rum in a bowl and mix well. Beat the butter in a mixing bowl at medium speed for 2 minutes or until creamy. Add the sugar gradually, beating constantly at medium speed for 5 to 7 minutes or until light and fluffy. Add the eggs one at a time, beating just until the yellow disappears after each addition.

With the mixer on low speed, add the flour mixture alternately with the pumpkin mixture, beating just until blended after each addition and beginning and ending with the flour mixture.

Spoon the batter into a greased and floured 10-inch tube pan or bundt pan. Bake in a preheated 325-degree oven for 80 to 90 minutes or until a wooden pick inserted near the center comes out clean. Cool in the pan for 10 minutes. Remove to a wire rack to cool completely.

To prepare the glaze, combine the butter, brown sugar, granulated sugar, cream and vanilla in a medium saucepan. Bring to a boil over medium heat, stirring constantly. Boil for 1 minute, stirring frequently. Drizzle over the cooled cake.

A favorite menu item served at Faculty and Staff Appreciation Luncheons.

Serves 12 to 16

Molasses Bars

2 1/2 cups all-purpose flour
1 teaspoon baking soda
1/2 teaspoon salt
1/2 teaspoon cinnamon
1/2 teaspoon nutmeg
1/2 teaspoon ginger
1 cup raisins
1 1/2 cups sugar
1/2 cup vegetable oil
1/2 cup molasses
2 eggs, lightly beaten
2 tablespoons sugar
2 tablespoons water

Combine the flour, baking soda, salt, cinnamon, nutmeg and ginger in a large bowl and mix well. Stir in the raisins. Combine 1 1/2 cups sugar, the oil, molasses and eggs in a bowl and mix well. Add to the flour mixture and mix well.

Spread the batter in a 10×15-inch baking pan.

Sprinkle 2 tablespoons sugar over the prepared layer and then sprinkle with the water. Pat lightly to ensure that the sugar is covered by the water. Bake in a preheated 350-degree oven for 25 to 30 minutes or until the bars test done. Cool in the pan on a wire rack. Cut into bars. Store in an airtight container.

Makes 2 dozen bars

Cheesy Apple Dapple Squares

1 1/2 cups all-purpose flour
1 1/2 cups graham cracker crumbs
1 cup packed brown sugar
3/4 cup (1 1/2 sticks) butter or margarine, softened
1/2 teaspoon baking soda
1 1/2 cups (6 ounces) shredded extra-sharp
    Cheddar cheese
4 cups sliced peeled Granny Smith apples
3/4 cup granulated sugar
Cinnamon to taste
1/2 cup chopped pecans

Combine the flour, graham cracker crumbs, brown sugar, butter and baking soda in a food processor and pulse until crumbly. Reserve 1/2 cup of the crumb mixture. Pat the remaining crumb mixture over the bottom of an ungreased 9×13-inch baking pan.

Sprinkle the cheese over the prepared layer. Layer with the apples and granulated sugar. Sprinkle with cinnamon, the remaining crumb mixture and pecans in the order listed. Bake in a preheated 350-degree oven for 35 minutes. Cool in the pan on a wire rack. Cut into squares. Store in an airtight container.

Makes 2 to 3 dozen squares

Cowboy Cookies

2 cups all-purpose flour
1 teaspoon baking soda
1/2 teaspoon baking powder
1/2 teaspoon salt
1 cup (2 sticks) butter or margarine, softened
1 cup granulated sugar
1 cup packed brown sugar
2 eggs
2 teaspoons vanilla extract
3 cups (18 ounces) chocolate chips
2 cups old-fashioned rolled oats
2 cups pecan halves or chopped pecans

Mix the flour, baking soda, baking powder and salt together. Beat the butter, granulated sugar, brown sugar and eggs in a mixing bowl until creamy. Add the flour mixture and mix until blended. Beat in the vanilla. Stir in the chocolate chips, oats and pecans.

Shape the dough by one-fourth cupfuls into balls. Arrange eight balls at a time on an ungreased cookie sheet. Bake in a preheated 350-degree oven for 12 to 15 minutes or until light brown. Cool on the cookie sheet for 2 minutes. Remove to a wire rack to cool completely. Store in an airtight container.

These may also be made into bars. A favorite of the Ravens' football teams and coaches.

Makes 2 dozen cookies

Originally published in *Raving Recipes.*

Ginger Bends

2 cups all-purpose flour
2 teaspoons baking soda
1 teaspoon ginger
1 teaspoon nutmeg
1 teaspoon cinnamon
1 teaspoon ground cloves

1 cup sugar
3/4 cup (1 1/2 sticks) butter, softened
1/4 cup molasses
1 egg
1/2 cup sugar

Mix the flour, baking soda, ginger, nutmeg, cinnamon and cloves together. Beat 1 cup sugar and the butter in a mixing bowl until creamy. Add the molasses and egg and beat until smooth. Blend in the flour mixture.

Pour 1/2 cup sugar in a shallow dish. Shape the dough into balls and coat with the sugar. Arrange 2 inches apart on a cookie sheet lined with baking parchment. Bake in a preheated 350-degree oven for 8 to 10 minutes or until crisp around the edges. Cool on the cookie sheet for 2 minutes. Remove to a wire rack to cool completely. Store in an airtight container.

Makes 4 dozen cookies

Cranberry Tart

1/2 cup walnuts, chopped
2 cups fresh cranberries
1 1/2 cups sugar
1 cup all-purpose flour

1/4 cup (1/2 stick) butter, softened
2 eggs
1/2 teaspoon almond extract
1/4 teaspoon salt

Layer the walnuts, cranberries and 1/2 cup of the sugar in the order listed in a greased 9-inch springform pan. Combine the remaining 1 cup sugar, the flour, butter, eggs, flavoring and salt in a mixing bowl and beat until a stiff batter forms.

Drop the batter by spoonfuls over the prepared layers. Bake in a preheated 350-degree oven for 40 minutes. Garnish with fresh cranberries.

Serves 8 to 10

Old-Fashioned Pecan Pie

Pie Pastry
1 cup all-purpose flour
$1/2$ teaspoon salt
$1/3$ cup shortening
2 tablespoons plus 2 teaspoons milk

Pecan Filling
4 eggs
$1 1/2$ cups light corn syrup
$3/4$ cup sugar
1 tablespoon butter, melted
1 teaspoon vanilla extract
$1/2$ teaspoon salt
$1 1/2$ cups pecan halves

To prepare the pastry, mix the flour and salt in a bowl. Cut in the shortening until the consistency of coarse meal using two knives or a pastry blender. Add just enough of the milk until the dough adheres, tossing lightly with a fork; do not beat. Roll the dough on a lightly floured surface and fit into a 9-inch pie plate. Crimp or flute the edges. Chill for 1 hour.

To prepare the filling, lightly beat the eggs in a bowl. Stir in the corn syrup, sugar, butter, vanilla and salt. Arrange the pecan halves over the bottom of the prepared pastry. Add just enough of the filling mixture to reach the top of the pie plate; there may be slightly more than needed.

Place the pie in a preheated 400 degree oven. Reduce the temperature to 350 degrees and bake for 45 to 60 minutes or until firm in the center. Cool on a wire rack for 2 hours or longer before serving.

Serves 6 to 8

Sour Cream Apple Pie

Pie
1 egg
1 cup sour cream, at room temperature
3/4 cup sugar
2 tablespoons all-purpose flour
1/2 teaspoon vanilla extract
Dash of salt
2 1/4 cups sliced peeled Granny Smith apples
1/4 teaspoon grated lemon zest
1 unbaked (9-inch) pie shell

Crumb Topping and Assembly
1/2 cup sugar
1/3 cup all-purpose flour
3/4 teaspoon cinnamon
1/4 cup (1/2 stick) butter

To prepare the pie, whisk the egg in a bowl until blended. Stir in the sour cream, sugar, flour, vanilla and salt. Fold in the apples and lemon zest. Spread in the pie shell.

Bake in a preheated 450-degree oven for 10 minutes. Reduce the oven temperature to 350 degrees and bake for 25 to 30 minutes longer or until the crust is golden brown. Maintain the oven temperature.

To prepare the topping, mix the sugar, flour and cinnamon in a small bowl. Cut in the butter until crumbly. Sprinkle over the pie and bake for 15 minutes longer. Remove to a wire rack to cool slightly. Serve warm or chill, covered, in the refrigerator.

Serves 8

Baked Pears with Blue Cheese and Port

    4 Bosc or Bartlett pears
    1/2 cup port
    1/2 cup honey
    1/4 cup crumbled blue cheese

Peel the pears. Cut the pears into halves and remove the core. Arrange the pears cut side up in a baking dish. Pour the wine over the pears and drizzle with the honey.

Bake in a preheated 350-degree oven for 30 minutes or until tender, basting with the pan juices occasionally. Remove from the oven and sprinkle 1 1/2 teaspoons of the cheese in the center of each pear half. Bake for 1 minute longer or until the cheese just begins to melt. Serve warm.

Serves 4

As polished heirloom silver gleams by candlelight amid arrangements of fresh greenery carefully selected from fall gardens, Southerners prepare their homes and their hearts for the holidays. Preparations are also underway on Ravenscroft's campus to embrace time-honored celebrations that are at the heart of the School's festive holiday season.

With an attractive, temperate climate to welcome them, many travel to the Raleigh area to enjoy the Thanksgiving holiday with their families. What better time to welcome them to our campus? For many years Ravenscroft School has hosted "Grandparents and Special Friends Day" during Thanksgiving week. On this memorable day, younger students proudly welcome grandparents and special friends to their classrooms and then lead them, walking hand-in-hand, to Thanksgiving Chapel. Time seems to stand still as students of all ages gather to give thanks through voice and instrument for the bounties of the season. Following Thanksgiving break, a series of string, choral, and band concerts not only showcase our students' musical talents, they also celebrate the diversity of beliefs and traditions among Ravenscroft families. This season of celebration culminates with the All School Chapel service where students participate in a program of holiday music and drama that embraces the School's Judeo-Christian tradition.

Throughout the year, but especially during the holiday season, parents welcome the opportunity to honor the School's faculty and staff at appreciation luncheons, where tantalizing dishes are lovingly prepared by volunteers and served amid attractive, themed decorations. Some of the most popular dishes served at these luncheons are included throughout this cookbook. In the following collection of recipes to honor this season of "Celebrations," you will find Wild Rice Dressing, Baked Apple and Cranberry Crisp, Holiday Citrus Salad, and Almond Crunch. These offerings, along with the many others contained in these pages, are sure to engender rave reviews at your holiday table and will enhance your family celebrations with flavor and good cheer.

Celebrations

Chapter Index

Three-Cheese Breakfast Strata

Overnight Potato Rolls

Caramelized French Toast

Noodle Kugel

Moravian Sugar Cake

Heavenly Scallops in Dijon Cream Sauce

Blue Cheese Ball

Baked Brie with Cranberries

Pepper Jelly and Brie Tartlets

Petite Potato Pancakes

Corn and Crab Soup

Roasted Winter Squash Soup

Ambrosia

Holiday Citrus Salad

Company Salad with Raspberry Vinaigrette

Warm Balsamic Mushroom Salad

Beef Tenderloin with Cabernet Au Jus

Beef Fillets with Marsala Sauce

Southern Sweet-and-Sour Brisket

Stuffed Pork Tenderloins

Apricot-Glazed Pork Loin

Casserole Saint Jacques

Honeyed Carrot Coins

Carrot Soufflé

White Cheddar au Gratin Potatoes

Mashed Turnip with Carrots and Orange

Wild Rice Dressing

Baked Apple and Cranberry Crisp

Old Southern Apple Cake

Red Velvet Cake

Almond Crunch

Cranberry Bars

Holiday Snickerdoodles

Pumpkin Mousse Pie

White Chocolate Raspberry Cheesecake

Eggnog Bavarian

Menus

Thanksgiving Dinner

Roasted Winter Squash Soup

Turkey

Mashed Turnip with Carrots & Orange

Baked Apple and Cranberry Crisp

Pumpkin Mousse Pie

*2006 Tobacco Road Pinot Noir,
Russian River Valley*

Home-style Hanukkah Dinner

Petite Potato Pancakes

Southern Sweet-and-Sour Brisket

Noodle Kugel

Honeyed Carrot Coins

Old Southern Apple Cake

Christmas Eve Dinner

Corn and Crab Soup

Company Salad with Raspberry Vinaigrette

Beef Tenderloin with Cabernet Au Jus

White Cheddar au Gratin Potatoes

Red Velvet Cake

*2005 Tobacco Road Cabernet Sauvignon
Private Reserve, Napa Valley*

Christmas Morning Brunch

Ambrosia

Three-Cheese Breakfast Strata

Moravian Sugar Cake

Ring in the New Year

Pepper Jelly and Brie Tartlets

Warm Balsamic Mushroom Salad

Beef Fillets with Marsala Sauce

Overnight Potato Rolls

White Chocolate Raspberry Cheesecake

*2005 Tobacco Road Cabernet
Sauvignon "Vitality," Napa Valley*

Three-Cheese Breakfast Strata

Butter for coating
1/2 to 1 dry loaf French bread
6 tablespoons butter, melted
12 ounces Swiss cheese, shredded
8 ounces Monterey Jack cheese, shredded
4 large green onions, chopped
9 slices ham, coarsely chopped
8 to 10 eggs
1 3/4 to 2 1/2 cups milk
1 tablespoon Dijon mustard
1 1/2 cups sour cream
1 cup (4 ounces) grated Parmesan cheese

Coat a 9×13-inch baking dish with butter. Break enough of the bread loaf into pieces to cover the bottom of the prepared baking dish and drizzle with melted butter. Layer with the Swiss cheese, Monterey Jack cheese, green onions and ham.

Whisk eight of the eggs, 1 3/4 cups of the milk and the Dijon mustard in a bowl until blended and pour over the bread pieces. If the bread pieces are not immersed over halfway in the egg mixture, whisk the remaining two eggs and 3/4 cup milk and add enough of the egg mixture to the baking dish to cover. Chill, covered, for 8 to 10 hours.

Let stand at room temperature for 30 minutes. Bake, covered, in a preheated 325-degree oven for 1 hour. Spread the sour cream over the baked layer and sprinkle with the Parmesan cheese. Bake, uncovered, for 10 to 15 minutes longer or until the Parmesan cheese begins to melt.

Feel free to substitute whatever cheese, meat, or bread you happen to have on hand.

Serves 12 to 16

Overnight Potato Rolls

1 envelope dry yeast
1 teaspoon sugar
1 1/2 cups warm (105- to 115-degree) potato water
    (reserved from boiling potatoes)
1 cup mashed cooked potatoes
2/3 cup sugar
2/3 cup shortening
2 eggs, lightly beaten
1 1/4 teaspoons salt
7 cups all-purpose flour

Dissolve the yeast and 1 teaspoon sugar in the warm potato water in a large bowl and mix well. Add the potatoes, 2/3 cup sugar, the shortening, eggs and salt and stir until blended. Add 3 1/2 cups of the flour and stir until smooth. Gradually add the remaining 3 1/2 cups flour, stirring after each addition until blended or use a durable mixer.

Knead the dough on a lightly floured surface for 3 to 5 minutes. Place the dough in a greased bowl, turning to coat the surface. Chill, covered loosely with plastic wrap, for 12 to 24 hours or until doubled in bulk. Punch the dough down.

Roll 3/4 inch thick on a lightly floured surface. Cut into 3-inch rounds or the size of your choice using a cutter. Arrange the rounds on a baking sheet. Let rise, covered, for 2 hours. Bake in a preheated 400-degree oven for 10 to 13 minutes or until light golden brown.

Makes 30 (3-inch) rolls

Caramelized French Toast

1 1/2 cups packed brown sugar
3/4 cup (1 1/2 sticks) butter
1/4 cup plus 2 teaspoons light
   corn syrup
1 loaf French bread, cut diagonally
   into 10 (1-inch) slices

1 1/2 cups milk
4 eggs, lightly beaten
1 teaspoon vanilla extract
1/4 teaspoon salt
1 tablespoon granulated sugar
1 1/2 teaspoons cinnamon

Combine the brown sugar, butter and corn syrup in a saucepan. Cook over medium heat for 5 minutes or until bubbly, stirring constantly. Pour into a greased 9×13-inch baking pan. Layer with the bread slices. Whisk the milk, eggs, vanilla and salt in a bowl until blended and pour over the prepared layers. Chill, covered with foil, for 8 to 10 hours. Turn the bread slices over, using a sharp knife to cut the caramel. Sprinkle with a mixture of the granulated sugar and cinnamon. Bake in a preheated 350-degree oven for 45 minutes.

Serves 8 to 10

Noodle Kugel

1 cup apricot nectar
4 ounces cream cheese, softened
1/2 cup cottage cheese
1/2 cup sugar
6 tablespoons butter, melted
1/4 cup milk
3 eggs, beaten

1 teaspoon vanilla extract
16 ounces egg noodles
1 (8-ounce) jar apricot jam
1 cup cornflakes, crushed
1/2 cup (1 stick) butter, melted
1/4 cup sugar
1/4 teaspoon cinnamon

Beat the apricot nectar, cream cheese, cottage cheese, 1/2 cup sugar, 6 tablespoons butter, the milk, eggs and vanilla in a mixing bowl until blended. Spread just enough over the bottom of a greased 9×13-inch baking dish or foil pan to coat. Cook the pasta using the package directions and drain. Spread in the prepared baking dish. Pour the remaining apricot nectar mixture over the pasta and smooth with a spatula. Drop the jam by spoonfuls over the top.

Mix the cornflakes, 1/2 cup butter, 1/4 cup sugar and the cinnamon in a bowl. Sprinkle over the top. Bake, covered, in a preheated 350-degree oven for 45 to 60 minutes or until light brown.

Serves 8 to 10

Moravian Sugar Cake

1 1/2 cups warm (105- to 115-degree) potato water
    (reserved from boiling potatoes)
1 cup mashed cooked potatoes
3/4 cup (1 1/2 sticks) butter or shortening
3/4 cup plus 2 tablespoons granulated sugar
4 to 5 cups all-purpose flour or bread flour
2 teaspoons salt
2 envelopes dry yeast
2 eggs, lightly beaten
1 1/2 cups packed brown sugar
1/2 teaspoon cinnamon
3/4 cup (1 1/2 sticks) butter

Combine the potato water, potatoes, 3/4 cup butter and the granulated sugar in a bowl and mix well. Mix 4 cups of the flour, the salt and yeast in a large bowl. Add the potato mixture and eggs and mix until the consistency of heavy muffin batter, adding the remaining 1 cup flour if needed for the desired consistency.

Place the dough in a lightly greased bowl, turning to coat the surface. Let rise, covered, in a warm place (such as a cool oven with the light on) until doubled in bulk. Punch the dough down and spread in three lightly greased 9x9-inch baking pans. Let rise until doubled in bulk. Pierce holes in the dough.

Mix the brown sugar and cinnamon in a bowl and sprinkle evenly over the tops. Cut 3/4 cup butter into small pieces and sprinkle 1/4 cup of the butter over each cake. Bake on the bottom oven rack in a preheated 375-degree oven for 10 minutes. Move the cakes to the top oven rack and bake for 10 minutes longer. Cool in the pans on a wire rack. Freeze for future use if desired.

Makes 3 cakes

A Moravian Church tradition enjoyed for generations.

Heavenly Scallops in Dijon Cream Sauce

10 slices bacon
20 large sea scallops
1 cup heavy whipping cream
2 tablespoons Dijon mustard, or to taste
2 tablespoons maple syrup
Salt and pepper to taste

Arrange the bacon slices in a single layer on a baking sheet. Bake in a preheated 350-degree oven for 8 minutes or until golden brown but not crisp. Cut each slice crosswise into halves and let stand until cool. Wrap each bacon piece around one scallop and secure with one or more wooden picks. At this point the scallops may be stored in the refrigerator for up to 6 hours. Arrange the scallops on a baking sheet. Bake in a preheated 400-degree oven for 10 minutes or until the scallops are opaque and slightly firm.

Bring the cream to a boil in a saucepan and boil for 3 minutes or until reduced by one-fourth, stirring frequently to prevent the cream from scorching. Stir in the Dijon mustard and syrup. Bring to a boil and boil for 3 minutes or until thickened and of a sauce consistency. Season with salt and pepper. Reduce the heat to a simmer to keep warm.

Spoon the warm sauce on serving plates. Arrange the scallops evenly over the sauce and discard the wooden picks. Garnish with chopped chives or chopped green onions.

Makes 20 hors d'oeuvre servings or 4 first-course servings

Blue Cheese Ball

6 ounces cream cheese, softened
6 ounces blue cheese, crumbled and
    at room temperature
6 ounces sharp Cheddar cheese, shredded and
    at room temperature
2 teaspoons Worcestershire sauce
2 teaspoons onion juice
2 dashes of garlic salt
Finely chopped pecans or other nuts, sunflower seeds
    or minced parsley

Combine the cream cheese, blue cheese, Cheddar cheese, Worcestershire sauce, onion juice and garlic salt in a bowl and mix well. Shape into a ball. Coat with pecans.

Chill, wrapped in plastic wrap, until firm. Serve with assorted party crackers and/or fresh vegetables.

Makes 1 large cheese ball

Baked Brie with Cranberries

1 (13- to 16-ounce) round Brie cheese
1 (16-ounce) can whole cranberry sauce
1/4 cup packed brown sugar
2 tablespoons spiced rum
1/2 teaspoon nutmeg
1/4 cup chopped pecans

Remove the rind from the top of the Brie and arrange in a shallow baking dish. Mix the cranberry sauce, brown sugar, rum and nutmeg in a bowl. Stir in the pecans.

Spoon over the top of the Brie round. Bake in a preheated 500-degree oven until the cheese begins to melt. Serve warm with assorted party crackers.

Serves 8 to 10

Pepper Jelly and Brie Tartlets

1 (8-ounce) Brie cheese
30 frozen miniature phyllo shells
1/2 cup pepper jelly

Freeze the cheese for 30 minutes to make slicing easier. Cut the cheese into 1/2-inch pieces. Arrange the phyllo shells on a baking sheet and place the cheese pieces in the shells.

Bake in a preheated 375-degree oven for 10 minutes or until the cheese melts. Remove from the oven and spoon the pepper jelly evenly over the melted cheese. Serve immediately.

Makes 30 tartlets

This is a sophisticated, easy-to-prepare twist on the old staple cream cheese with pepper jelly. It is great for a cocktail party and looks like you went to a lot of effort. Use your favorite pepper jelly—ancho chili and red bell pepper are great choices.

Petite Potato Pancakes

2 Idaho, russet or starchy baking potatoes
1/2 cup grated onion
3 eggs, beaten
1 tablespoon all-purpose flour
1 1/2 teaspoons salt
1/2 teaspoon baking powder
Dash of pepper
1/4 cup vegetable oil

Grate enough of the potatoes using a medium hand grater or process in a food processor to measure 2 cups. Drain and press out any excess moisture. Combine the potatoes, onion and eggs in a bowl and mix well. Stir in a mixture of the flour, salt, baking powder and pepper.

Heat the oil in a skillet until hot. Drop the potato mixture by tablespoonfuls into the hot oil and fry until the pancakes are brown on both sides, turning once. Drain on paper towels. Arrange the pancakes in a single layer on a baking sheet and reheat in a preheated 350-degree oven for 10 minutes. Serve warm with sour cream or caviar. Fry in advance and reheat just before serving, if desired.

Makes 30 pancakes

These are the ever-popular Hanukkah treats in an appetizer version. The pancakes are crisp and a delicious tradition.

Corn and Crab Soup

1/4 cup finely chopped onion
Butter for sautéing
3 ears of corn, or 1 1/2 cups thawed frozen corn kernels
1 tablespoon olive oil
5 tablespoons butter
5 tablespoons all-purpose flour
2 1/2 cups milk
2 cups chicken broth
3/4 cup fresh crab meat, shells removed and meat flaked
Salt and black pepper to taste
1/2 cup heavy cream
Dash of cayenne pepper
4 slices applewood-smoked bacon, crisp-cooked and
    crumbled (optional)

Sauté the onion in butter in a skillet until tender. Remove the corn kernels from the cob using a sharp knife. This should measure about 1 1/2 cups. Sauté the corn in the olive oil in a skillet over medium-high heat until tender.

Melt 5 tablespoons butter in a Dutch oven and stir in the flour until blended. Cook until bubbly, stirring constantly. Whisk in the milk and broth until blended. Cook for about 10 minutes or until thickened, whisking frequently. Stir in the onion, corn, crab meat, salt, black pepper, cream and cayenne pepper.

Bring to a boil and then reduce the heat. Simmer for 5 minutes and stir in the bacon. Ladle into soup bowls and serve immediately.

Serves 4

Roasted Winter Squash Soup

1 butternut squash
1 acorn squash
2 tablespoons butter
2 tablespoons olive oil
1 onion, chopped
1 carrot, chopped
Salt and pepper to taste
6 cups chicken or vegetable broth
1 tablespoon grated fresh ginger, or
    1 teaspoon ground ginger
Dash of grated nutmeg

Cut the butternut squash and acorn squash into halves and remove the seeds. Arrange the squash cut side down on a baking sheet lined with foil. Roast in a preheated 375-degree oven for 1 hour. Cool slightly. Remove the pulp, discarding the skin. Mash the pulp in a bowl.

Heat the butter and olive oil in a skillet until the butter melts. Add the onion and carrot and season with salt and pepper. Cook over low heat for 10 to 15 minutes or until the vegetables are tender but not brown, stirring occasionally. Stir in the squash, broth and ginger.

Bring to a boil and then reduce the heat. Simmer for 20 minutes, stirring occasionally. Stir in the nutmeg and season with salt and pepper. Process the soup in batches in a blender until puréed or use an immersion blender to purée. Ladle into soup bowls and serve immediately.

This recipe may also be prepared using two butternut squash or two acorn squash.

Serves 6 to 8

Ambrosia

8 cups assorted sliced fresh fruit
such as grapes, strawberries
kiwifruit, bananas, blackberries
and/or cherries

1 (16-ounce) can mandarin
oranges, drained
Juice of 1 large lemon
1/2 cup sweetened shredded coconut

Toss the assorted fresh fruit and mandarin oranges with the lemon juice in a large bowl. Sprinkle with the coconut and mix gently. Serve immediately or chill, covered, until serving time.

Serves 8

Having trouble convincing your family to eat enough fresh fruit? Try offering chunks of fresh fruit with a simple and easy dip consisting of marshmallow creme blended with strawberry cream cheese. Problem solved.

Holiday Citrus Salad

1/4 cup orange juice
3 1/2 tablespoons olive oil
2 tablespoons white wine vinegar
1 tablespoon grated orange zest
1 teaspoon sugar
Salt and pepper to taste

6 cups mixed baby greens
2 (15-ounce) cans mandarin
oranges, drained
1/2 cup dried cranberries
1/4 cup pecans, toasted

Whisk the orange juice, olive oil, vinegar, orange zest and sugar in a bowl until combined. Season with salt and pepper.

Toss the greens with the mandarin oranges and cranberries in a salad bowl. Add the dressing and mix to coat. Sprinkle with the pecans and serve immediately.

A favorite menu item at Faculty and Staff Appreciation Luncheons.

Serves 6 to 8

To make preparation even easier, use a commercially prepared salad dressing such as a raspberry vinaigrette or any dressing with a sweet-and-sour flavor.

Company Salad with Raspberry Vinaigrette

Raspberry Vinaigrette
1/2 cup vegetable oil
1/4 cup raspberry vinegar
1 tablespoon honey
1/2 teaspoon grated orange zest
1/4 teaspoon salt
1/8 teaspoon pepper

Salad
1 head Bibb lettuce, trimmed and torn into
 bite-size pieces
1 small head romaine, trimmed and torn into
 bite-size pieces
8 ounces fresh baby spinach, trimmed and
 torn into bite-size pieces
Sections of 2 oranges
2 red Delicious apples, sliced or cut into chunks
1 kiwifruit, thinly sliced
1/2 cup coarsely chopped walnuts, toasted

To prepare the vinaigrette, combine the oil, vinegar, honey, orange zest, salt and pepper in a jar with a tight-fitting lid and seal tightly. Shake to mix. Chill in the refrigerator.

To prepare the salad, toss the Bibb lettuce, romaine, spinach, orange sections, apples, kiwifruit and walnuts in a large salad bowl. Add the dressing just before serving and mix well.

A favorite menu item served at Faculty and Staff Appreciation Luncheons.

Serves 8

Warm Balsamic Mushroom Salad

2 tablespoons olive oil
2 large shallots, thinly sliced
8 ounces white button mushrooms, sliced
4 ounces shiitake mushrooms, stems removed and sliced
4 ounces cremini mushrooms, sliced
2 tablespoons olive oil
Salt and pepper to taste
1 tablespoon balsamic vinegar
6 cups mixed baby greens
2 tablespoons olive oil
2 teaspoons balsamic vinegar
4 ounces Gorgonzola cheese or
    other blue cheese, crumbled

Heat 2 tablespoons olive oil in a large skillet over medium-high heat. Add the shallots and cook just until the shallots begin to brown and caramelize. Add the mushrooms, 2 tablespoons olive oil, salt and pepper and sauté for 5 minutes or until the mushrooms are tender. Stir in 1 tablespoon vinegar.

Toss the greens with 2 tablespoons olive oil and 2 teaspoons vinegar in a large salad bowl. Season with salt and pepper. Arrange the greens evenly on a rectangular or narrow oval platter. Spoon the warm mushroom mixture over the center of the greens and sprinkle the blue cheese over the top. Serve warm.

Great with steak or beef tenderloin.

Serves 6 to 8

Beef Tenderloin with Cabernet Au Jus

Tenderloin
2 tablespoons olive oil
2 tablespoons crushed pepper
2 tablespoons chopped fresh thyme
2 tablespoons kosher salt
1 (4- to 6-pound) beef tenderloin, trimmed

Cabernet Sauce
1 1/2 cups cabernet sauvignon
2 tablespoons balsamic vinegar
1 shallot, chopped
1 tablespoon chopped fresh thyme
1 garlic clove, chopped
1 1/2 cups beef broth
2 tablespoons butter

To prepare the tenderloin, mix the olive oil, pepper, thyme and salt in a small bowl. Rub over the surface of the tenderloin. Place the tenderloin in a large glass dish and marinate, covered, in the refrigerator for 2 to 12 hours.

Brown the tenderloin on all sides in a large skillet or roasting pan over medium-high heat. Arrange the tenderloin on a rack in a roasting pan. Roast in a preheated 425-degree oven to the desired degree of doneness or until a meat thermometer registers 145 degrees for medium-rare. Let stand, covered, for 5 to 10 minutes before slicing.

To prepare the sauce, combine the wine, vinegar, shallot, thyme and garlic in a saucepan. Cook over medium heat until the mixture is reduced by half, stirring occasionally. Add the broth and cook until reduced by half again. Strain the sauce and return to the saucepan. Whisk in the butter. Simmer just until heated through. Cover to keep warm.

Slice the tenderloin into 1/2-inch slices. Arrange on a platter and drizzle with the sauce. Serve immediately.

Serves 8 to 10

This is a wonderful entrée for entertaining. You can sear the tenderloin in advance and roast it when your guests arrive. The sauce may be prepared in advance and reheated just before serving.

Beef Fillets with Marsala Sauce

4 (6- to 8-ounce) beef tenderloin fillets
1/2 teaspoon salt
1/2 teaspoon pepper
1 teaspoon olive oil
1 teaspoon butter
2 cups marsala
1 cup low-sodium chicken broth
1 (5-ounce) can fat-free evaporated milk
1/4 teaspoon Dijon mustard

Sprinkle the fillets with the salt and pepper. Heat the olive oil and butter in a large skillet over medium-high heat until the butter melts. Add the fillets and cook for approximately 6 minutes on each side or until the desired degree of doneness.

Remove the fillets to a platter and cover to keep warm, reserving the pan drippings. Add the wine and broth to the reserved pan drippings. Cook for 20 minutes or until reduced by half. Stir in the evaporated milk and Dijon mustard. Cook over low heat until slightly thickened, stirring occasionally. Drizzle over the fillets on a platter. Serve immediately.

Serves 4

Southern Sweet-and-Sour Brisket

1 teaspoon minced garlic
1 (3- to 5-pound) beef brisket
Salt and freshly ground pepper to taste
2 tablespoons vegetable oil
2 large sweet onions, sliced
1/2 cup red wine
1 (14-ounce) can beef broth
1 cup chili sauce
1/2 cup apple cider vinegar
1/2 cup packed dark brown sugar
1 teaspoon dry mustard
1 bay leaf

Rub the garlic over the surface of the brisket and sprinkle with salt and pepper. Heat 1 tablespoon of the oil in a Dutch oven or roasting pan over medium heat. Sear the brisket in the hot oil for 3 minutes per side or until brown. Remove the brisket to a platter, reserving the pan drippings. Heat the remaining 1 tablespoon oil with the reserved pan drippings and add the onions.

Cook for 5 minutes or until the onions are caramelized, stirring occasionally. Add the wine and broth and stir with a wooden spoon to release any browned bits on the bottom of the Dutch oven. Add the chili sauce, vinegar, brown sugar, dry mustard and bay leaf and mix well. Return the brisket to the Dutch oven and spoon the sauce over the top.

Bake, covered, in a preheated 350-degree oven for 2 hours or until fork-tender. Maintain the oven temperature. Remove the brisket to a platter and slice across the grain, reserving the sauce. Arrange the slices overlapping in the Dutch oven and spoon the sauce over the top. Bake, covered, for 1 hour longer. Discard the bay leaf before serving.

For the best flavor, allow the brisket to cool and then chill for 8 to 10 hours. Reheat, covered, in a preheated 300-degree oven for 30 minutes.

Serves 6 to 8

Stuffed Pork Tenderloins

2 (1-pound) pork tenderloins, butterflied
1/2 teaspoon salt
1/4 teaspoon pepper
1 (6-ounce) package pork-flavor stuffing mix
1 (24-ounce) jar applesauce
1 (10-ounce) jar cherry preserves

Lay the tenderloins open like a book on a hard work surface. Sprinkle the cut sides with the salt and pepper. Combine the stuffing mix and applesauce in a bowl and mix well. Spoon equal portions of the stuffing mixture down the center of each tenderloin. Bring the sides over the filling and secure with kitchen twine or wooden picks to form a log.

Arrange the tenderloins on a rack in a roasting pan. Spread the preserves evenly over the tops of the tenderloins. Bake, covered with foil, in a preheated 350-degree oven for 45 to 50 minutes. Remove the foil and bake for 10 to 15 minutes longer or until brown.

You may substitute pork loin for the pork tenderloin, but the baking time needs to be adjusted.

Serves 6 to 8

*A*sk the butcher to butterfly the pork tenderloin and run through the cubing machine once. This makes the tenderloin flat and even more tender.

Apricot-Glazed Pork Loin

1 (5- to 6-pound) pork loin roast
2 large garlic cloves, slivered
$1/2$ cup soy sauce
$1/2$ cup ketchup
$1/4$ cup lemon juice
2 garlic cloves, crushed
$1/2$ teaspoon pepper
2 cups apricot preserves

Make slits in the surface of the roast and insert the garlic slivers in the slits. Place the roast in a 9×13-inch baking dish. Mix the soy sauce, ketchup, lemon juice, pressed garlic and pepper in a bowl and pour over the roast. Marinate, covered, in the refrigerator for 8 to 10 hours, turning three or four times.

Arrange the roast on a rack in a shallow roasting pan, reserving the marinade. Baste with the reserved marinade. Roast in a preheated 325-degree oven for 2 hours, basting with the reserved marinade every 30 minutes and covering with foil if the roast begins to brown too quickly.

Heat the preserves in a saucepan until melted. Brush $3/4$ cup of the preserves over the top of the roast and roast for 30 minutes longer. Remove the roast to a serving platter and garnish with sprigs of parsley. Serve with the remaining warm preserves.

Serves 10

Casserole Saint Jacques

1 pound scallops
1 cup dry white wine
1 small onion, sliced
2 teaspoons lemon juice
1/2 teaspoon salt
1/4 cup (1/2 stick) butter or margarine
1/4 cup all-purpose flour
1 cup evaporated milk
2 ounces (or more) Gruyère cheese, grated
Dash of pepper
8 ounces crab meat, shells removed and meat flaked
8 ounces cooked shrimp, cut into bite-size pieces
1 1/2 cups soft bread crumbs
1 tablespoon butter, melted

Cut any large scallops into bite-size pieces. Combine the scallops, wine, onion, lemon juice and salt in a saucepan and bring to a boil. Reduce the heat and simmer for 5 minutes. Drain, reserving 1 cup of the pan juices.

Melt 1/4 cup butter in a saucepan and stir in the flour until blended. Cook until bubbly, stirring constantly. Add the evaporated milk and reserved 1 cup pan juices and mix well. Cook over medium heat until thickened, stirring constantly. Remove from the heat and stir in the cheese and pepper. Fold in the scallops, crab meat and shrimp.

Spoon into an 8x8-inch baking dish. Sprinkle with the bread crumbs and drizzle with 1 tablespoon butter. Bake in a preheated 350-degree oven for 25 minutes. You may prepare in advance and store, covered, in the refrigerator. Bake just before serving.

Serves 6

Honeyed Carrot Coins

1 1/2 cups sliced carrots
1/2 cup apple juice
1 tablespoon honey
1 teaspoon grated orange zest
1 teaspoon grated lemon zest
1 teaspoon butter or margarine
1/4 teaspoon salt (optional)

Combine the carrots and apple juice in a small saucepan. Cook, covered, over medium heat for 10 minutes or until the carrots are tender. Stir in the orange zest, lemon zest, butter and salt. Serve with a slotted spoon.

Serves 2

Carrot Soufflé

1 1/2 pounds carrots, peeled and cut into chunks
1 1/2 cups sugar
1 cup sour cream
1/2 cup (1 stick) butter or margarine
3 eggs
1/4 cup all-purpose flour
1 1/2 teaspoons baking powder
1/4 teaspoon cinnamon

Cook the carrots in boiling water in a saucepan for 20 to 25 minutes or until tender; drain. Process the carrots, sugar, sour cream, butter, eggs, flour, baking powder and cinnamon in batches in a food processor until smooth, scraping the side of the bowl as needed.

Spoon into a lightly greased 1 1/2-quart soufflé dish. Bake in a preheated 350-degree oven for 1 hour and 10 minutes or until set. Garnish with chopped pecans and serve immediately.

Serves 6 to 8

White Cheddar au Gratin Potatoes

3 pounds Yukon gold potatoes, peeled and cut into 1/8-inch rounds

2 teaspoons salt

1 teaspoon pepper

2 1/2 teaspoons dried tarragon

6 ounces sharp white Cheddar cheese, shredded

1 cup whipping cream

1 cup dry white wine

Layer the potatoes, salt, pepper, tarragon and cheese one-third at a time in a buttered 9×13-inch baking dish. Whisk the cream and wine in a bowl until blended and pour over the prepared layers. Bake in a preheated 400-degree oven for 1 hour or until the potatoes are golden brown and tender when pierced with a knife. Let stand for 5 minutes before serving.

Serves 12

Mashed Turnip with Carrots and Orange

1 small yellow or white turnip, peeled and cut into chunks

4 carrots, peeled and cut into chunks

3 tablespoons brown sugar

1 tablespoon butter

2 tablespoons frozen orange juice concentrate

Pinch of nutmeg

Salt and freshly ground pepper to taste

Cook the turnip and carrots in simmering water in separate saucepans until very tender; drain. Mash the turnip and carrots in separate bowls.

Combine the turnip, carrots, brown sugar, butter, orange juice concentrate, nutmeg, salt and pepper in a bowl and mix well. Spoon into a serving bowl and garnish with chopped parsley.

Serves 4 or more

Originally published in *Raving Recipes*.

Wild Rice Dressing

2 tablespoons butter
1 (16-ounce) package frozen pearl onions
4 1/2 cups canned vegetable broth
1 1/2 teaspoons dried thyme, crumbled
1 1/4 cups wild rice
1 1/4 cups long-grain white basmati rice
1 (6-ounce) package dried apricots, coarsely chopped
1 cup dried tart cherries
1 cup golden raisins or dried cranberries
1/4 cup (1/2 stick) butter, cut into chunks
1 cup pecans, toasted and chopped
Salt and pepper to taste

Melt 2 tablespoons butter in a large skillet over medium heat and add the onions. Sauté for 15 minutes or until the onions are brown.

Bring the broth and thyme to a boil in a large saucepan. Add the wild rice and return to a boil. Reduce the heat and simmer, covered, for 30 minutes. Stir in the white rice and simmer, covered, for 15 minutes longer or until most of the liquid is absorbed. Add the apricots, cherries and raisins and mix well.

Simmer, covered, for 3 minutes. Remove from the heat and stir in the onions and 1/4 cup butter. Mix in the pecans and season with salt and pepper. Spoon the dressing into a buttered 9×13-inch baking dish. Coat one side of a sheet of foil large enough to cover the baking dish with butter and place butter side down over the dressing. Bake in a preheated 350-degree oven for 30 minutes.

Make sure you use real wild rice and not a wild rice blend or the texture will be gummy. This is great with ham as well as poultry. A favorite menu item served at Faculty and Staff Appreciation Luncheons.

Serves 8 to 10

Baked Apple and Cranberry Crisp

3 cups chopped peeled apples
2 cups fresh cranberries
1 cup granulated sugar
1 3/4 cups quick-cooking oats

1/2 cup packed brown sugar
1/2 cup (1 stick) butter, melted
3/4 cup chopped pecans

Combine the apples, cranberries and granulated sugar in a bowl and mix well. Spread in a greased 9×13-inch baking dish. Combine the oats, brown sugar, butter and pecans and stir until crumbly. Sprinkle over the prepared layer. Bake in a preheated 350-degree oven for 1 hour. Serve warm.

A favorite menu item served at Faculty and Staff Appreciation Luncheons.

Serves 8 to 10

Old Southern Apple Cake

2 1/2 cups all-purpose flour
2 teaspoons baking powder
1 teaspoon salt
1 teaspoon baking soda
2 cups granulated sugar
1 1/4 cups vegetable oil
2 eggs

3 cups chopped apples
1 cup chopped walnuts or
    chopped pecans
1 tablespoon vanilla extract or
    rum extract
Confectioners' sugar for dusting

Sift the flour, baking powder, salt and baking soda into a bowl and mix well. Combine the granulated sugar, oil and eggs in a mixing bowl and beat until creamy. Add the dry ingredients mix well; the batter will be stiff. Stir in the apples, nuts and vanilla. Spread in a greased 9×13-inch cake pan. Bake in a preheated 350-degree oven for 1 hour or until the cake tests done. Cool in the pan on a wire rack. Serve dusted with confectioners' sugar as coffee cake or dessert. May be prepared in advance or frozen for future use, if desired.

Serves 15

*O*riginally published in *Raving Recipes.*

Red Velvet Cake

Cake

2 1/4 cups sifted cake flour
2 tablespoons (heaping) baking cocoa
1 teaspoon baking powder
1 teaspoon baking soda
1/2 teaspoon salt
1 cup buttermilk
2 tablespoons red food coloring
1 teaspoon vanilla extract
1 teaspoon vinegar
1 cup (2 sticks) butter, softened
1 1/2 cups sugar

Chocolate Filling

2 ounces unsweetened chocolate
2 tablespoons butter
1 (14-ounce) can sweetened
   condensed milk
1 teaspoon vanilla extract

Cream Cheese Frosting

16 ounces cream cheese, softened
1/2 cup (1 stick) butter, softened
1 teaspoon vanilla extract
2 cups sifted confectioners' sugar

To prepare the cake, sift the cake flour, baking cocoa, baking powder, baking soda and salt into a bowl and mix well. Mix the buttermilk, food coloring, vanilla and vinegar in a measuring cup. Cream the butter and sugar in a mixing bowl until light and fluffy. Add one-third of the buttermilk mixture to the creamed mixture and mix until blended. Add one-third of the dry ingredients to the creamed mixture and mix well. Alternately add the remaining buttermilk mixture and the remaining dry ingredients to the creamed mixture, mixing well after each addition and ending with the dry ingredients.

Spoon the batter into three greased and floured 9-inch cake pans. Bake in a preheated 350-degree oven for 20 minutes or until the layers test done. Cool in the pans for 10 minutes. Remove to a wire rack to cool completely.

To prepare the filling, heat the chocolate and butter in a double boiler over medium heat until melted. Stir in the condensed milk and vanilla. Cook until thickened; the filling is ready when the chocolate filling will barely drop off an overturned spoon. Spread one-half of the filling on one cake layer and arrange another cake layer over the filling. Spread the remainder of the filling on the second cake layer and top with the third cake layer.

To prepare the frosting, beat the cream cheese and butter in a mixing bowl until creamy. Blend in the vanilla. Add the confectioners' sugar and beat until of a spreading consistency. Spread over the top and side of the cake.

Serves 12

Almond Crunch

1 cup (2 sticks) butter
1 1/4 cups sugar
2 tablespoons corn syrup
2 tablespoons water
1 cup slivered almonds, toasted
2 cups (12 ounces) milk chocolate chips

Combine the butter, sugar, corn syrup and water in a heavy saucepan. Cook over medium heat to 300 degrees on a candy thermometer, brittle stage, stirring constantly. If you are not using a candy thermometer, take a spoon and drip one or two drops of the candy mixture into a glass of cold water. Feel the mixture in the water; if it is brittle it is ready. If it is still pliable, the mixture needs to cook longer. Watch for the color of the mixture to go from the original light yellow butter color to a tan caramel color, resembling the color of a baseball glove. Do not allow to become dark brown as this means it has burned.

Remove from the heat and quickly stir in the almonds. Immediately pour into a 9×11-inch heatproof dish or baking sheet lined with buttered foil. Sprinkle with the chocolate chips. Let stand for 5 minutes or until the chocolate is shiny and soft. Spread evenly over the toffee layer. Let stand until room temperature and then chill for 1 hour. Lift the candy out of the dish and remove the foil. Break into 1 1/2-inch pieces. Store in an airtight container.

A favorite menu item served at Faculty and Staff Appreciation Luncheons.

Makes 2 dozen pieces

Cranberry Bars

1 1/2 cups all-purpose flour
1 1/2 cups quick-cooking oats
3/4 cup packed brown sugar
1 teaspoon grated lemon zest
1/4 teaspoon baking soda
3/4 cup (1 1/2 sticks) butter, melted
1 (16-ounce) can whole cranberry sauce
1/4 cup chopped pecans or walnuts

Combine the flour, oats, brown sugar, lemon zest and baking soda in a bowl and mix well. Add the butter and mix until thoroughly combined. Reserve 1 cup of the oat mixture. Pat the remaining oat mixture over the bottom of an ungreased 9x13-inch baking pan. Bake in a preheated 350-degree oven for 20 minutes. Maintain the oven temperature.

Spread the cranberry sauce over the baked layer. Mix the pecans into the reserved 1 cup oat mixture and sprinkle over the prepared layers. Lightly pat the oat mixture into the cranberry sauce. Bake for 25 to 30 minutes or until golden brown. Cool in the pan on a wire rack and cut into bars. Store in an airtight container.

Makes 2 dozen bars

Holiday Snickerdoodles

1/4 cup tinted granulated sugar
1 teaspoon nutmeg
2 3/4 cups sifted all-purpose flour
1 1/2 cups granulated sugar
1 cup (2 sticks) butter, softened
2 eggs
2 teaspoons cream of tartar
1 teaspoon baking soda
1/2 teaspoon brandy extract
1/2 teaspoon rum extract
1/4 teaspoon salt

Combine the tinted sugar and nutmeg in a bowl and mix well. Chill for 20 minutes. Combine the flour, granulated sugar, butter, eggs, cream of tartar, baking soda, flavorings and salt in a mixing bowl. Beat at low speed for 2 to 4 minutes or until combined.

Shape the dough by rounded teaspoonfuls into 1-inch balls and coat with the tinted sugar mixture. Arrange 2 inches apart on an ungreased cookie sheet. Bake in a preheated 400-degree oven for 8 to 10 minutes or until light brown. Cool on the cookie sheet for 2 minutes. Remove to a wire rack to cool completely. Store in an airtight container.

Makes 7 dozen cookies

These have a great flavor reminiscent of eggnog.

Pumpkin Mousse Pie

Crunch Topping
1/4 cup (1/2 stick) salted butter
1 cup chopped pecans
1/2 cup sugar

Pie
1 baked (9-inch) pie shell
1 envelope unflavored gelatin
1/2 cup cold water
3/4 cup packed light brown sugar
1 (15-ounce) can pumpkin purée
1/4 cup milk
1 teaspoon cinnamon
3/4 teaspoon nutmeg
1/2 teaspoon salt
2 cups whipped cream

To prepare the topping, melt the butter in a heavy saucepan and stir in the pecans and sugar. Cook for 3 to 5 minutes or until the mixture is golden brown, stirring constantly. Spread on a sheet of foil and let stand until cool; crumble.

To prepare the pie, sprinkle 1 cup of the topping over the bottom of the pie shell. Sprinkle the gelatin over the water in a saucepan. Simmer over low heat until the gelatin dissolves. Remove from the heat and add the brown sugar. Stir until the brown sugar dissolves.

Combine the pumpkin, milk, cinnamon, nutmeg and salt in a bowl and mix until combined. Gradually blend in the gelatin mixture. Fold in 1 cup of the whipped cream. Spread the pumpkin filling in the prepared pie shell. Top with the remaining whipped cream and sprinkle with the remaining topping. Chill until serving time.

Serves 8 to 10

White Chocolate Raspberry Cheesecake

Graham Cracker Crust
Butter for coating
1/2 cup slivered almonds
1 cup graham cracker crumbs
1/4 cup sugar
1/4 cup (1/2 stick) butter, melted
1 teaspoon almond extract

White Chocolate-Raspberry Filling
32 ounces cream cheese, softened
2 cups sugar
6 eggs

2 cups sour cream
2 teaspoons vanilla extract
1/2 cup chopped white chocolate
1/2 cup raspberry jam
3 tablespoons water

Raspberry Topping
3/4 cup sour cream
1/4 cup raspberry jam
3 tablespoons sugar
1 tablespoon water
1/2 teaspoon vanilla extract

To prepare the crust, coat the bottom and side of a 10-inch springform pan with butter or spray with nonstick cooking spray. Wrap the bottom and side of the springform pan with two layers of foil. Spread the almonds in a single layer on a baking sheet. Toast in a preheated 350-degree oven for 5 to 10 minutes or until fragrant and light brown, gently shaking the baking sheet every 2 to 3 minutes. Maintain the oven temperature.

Mix the almonds, graham cracker crumbs and sugar in a bowl. Add 1/4 cup butter and the flavoring and mix well. Pat over the bottom of the prepared pan.

To prepare the filling, beat the cream cheese and sugar in a mixing bowl until smooth and fluffy. Add the eggs one at a time, mixing just until blended after each addition; do not overmix. Add the sour cream and vanilla and beat just until blended. Fold in the white chocolate. Spread the filling over the prepared layer. Mix the jam and water in a small bowl and drizzle in a spiral pattern over the top. Gently swirl in the jam, leaving swirls visible.

Place the springform pan in a larger baking pan and add enough water to the baking pan to measure 1 inch. Bake for 1 hour and 15 minutes or until set and light brown. Turn off the oven and let the cheesecake stand in the oven with the door closed for 1 hour. Remove to a wire rack to cool. Chill for 8 to 10 hours if possible. Run a sharp knife around the side of the cheesecake to loosen the side of the pan.

To prepare the topping, combine the sour cream, jam, sugar, water and vanilla in a bowl and mix well. Spread over the chilled layer. Garnish with white chocolate shavings. Store in the refrigerator until serving time.

Serves 12

Eggnog Bavarian

3 envelopes unflavored gelatin
3/4 cup cold water
1 cup eggnog
1/4 cup sugar
1/4 teaspoon nutmeg
3 cups eggnog
1 cup heavy whipping cream, whipped

Sprinkle the gelatin over the water in a bowl. Let stand until softened. Combine 1 cup eggnog, the sugar, nutmeg and gelatin mixture in a 2-quart saucepan. Cook over low heat until the gelatin dissolves, stirring occasionally. Stir in 3 cups eggnog.

Pour into a glass bowl and chill, covered, until thickened, whisking and scraping the side of the bowl occasionally. Do not allow the mixture to completely set. Fold in the whipped cream until incorporated and chill until firm. Spoon into dessert bowls.

Serves 8

When morning frost glistens on the campus green and trees stand bare against the frozen sky, the Ravenscroft community surrounds itself with warmth. In Lower School, children delight in learning about famous Americans born in winter months, celebrating the 100th day of school, exchanging valentines, and flying across playgrounds like snowflakes in the wind. Middle and Upper School students renew their dedication to studies as a new semester begins. They find exhilaration in winter sports, theatrical productions, art exhibits, community service projects, and countless other activities that allow them to learn, share, thrive, and grow, even when all of nature seems to lie dormant around them.

For Ravens of a certain generation, winter will always summon up memories of the School's Tucker Street campus and the remarkable Quonset hut, a structure built after World War II to expand space in a time of scarce finances. The Quonset hut housed two large classrooms that were heated by the crackling fires of potbelly stoves. Students of that era recall the unexpectedly warm and cozy feel of those classrooms, an atmosphere where children felt secure and quite at home. Other fond memories of Tucker Street include the George Washington Play and Mrs. Washington's Tea Party, first performed in the winter of 1938, which remained traditions at the School for many years.

The recipes that follow are sure to bring warmth to your table and comfort to your spirit throughout the winter months. We are especially pleased to be able to offer with our dessert selections the Sweet Potato Bread Pudding recipe from Raleigh's outstanding Second Empire Restaurant, owned by the family of two Ravenscroft alumni. We know you will enjoy the rich, hearty flavors of winter and the experience of sharing them with family and friends.

Winter
Warmth

Chapter Index

Country Egg and Sausage Pie

Breakfast Spice Bread

Sour Cream Corn Bread

Cheddar Muffins

Best-Ever White Bread

Chili Cheese Mexican Dip

Lentil Pâté

Swiss Almond Spread

Pigs in Cashmere Blankets

Spicy Won Tons

Red and White Chicken Chili

Red Hot Chili for a Crowd

Sausage and Corn Chowder

Swiss Potato Soup

Roasted Tomato Soup

Crunchy Orange Almond Salad

Blue Cheese Coleslaw

Burgundy Beef Tips

Beef Bourguignon

Citrus-Marinated Pork Tenderloin

Herb-Roasted Loin of Pork

North Carolina Barbecue

Blackened Chicken Cordon Bleu

Chicken Caprese with Tomato Basil Sauce

Pan-Seared Sea Scallops in
    Champagne Cream Sauce

Shrimp and Grits Casserole

Linguini with Sun-Dried Tomatoes
    and Olives

Pasta Shells with Mushrooms and
    Radicchio

Hoppin' John

Sautéed Collard Greens

White Corn Risotto

Frosted Fudge Brownies

Butterscotch Pie

Mixed Berry Pie with Pecan-Orange
    Lattice Crust

Cranberry Swirl Cheesecake

Second Empire Sweet Potato Bread
    Pudding

Pots de Crème

Menus

"New" Year's Traditions

Sausage and Corn Chowder

Herb-Roasted Loin of Pork

Hoppin' John

Sautéed Collard Greens

Cranberry Swirl Cheesecake

*2005 Tobacco Road Cabernet Sauvignon
Private Reserve, Napa Valley*

Romantic Valentine's Dinner

Roasted Tomato Soup

Pan-Seared Scallops in Champagne
Cream Sauce

White Corn Risotto

Pots de Crème

*2006 Tobacco Road Pinot Noir,
Russian River Valley*

Mardi Gras Party

Spicy Won Tons

Blackened Chicken Cordon Bleu

Crunchy Orange Almond Salad

Second Empire Sweet Potato
Bread Pudding

Après Ski

Swiss Almond Spread

Red and White Chicken Chili

Sour Cream Corn Bread

Butterscotch Pie

*2006 Tobacco Road Syrah,
Santa Barbara*

ACC Tournament Party

Chili Cheese Mexican Dip

North Carolina Barbecue

Blue Cheese Coleslaw

Frosted Fudge Brownies

Country Egg and Sausage Pie

2 (9-inch) pie shells
1 pound hot or mild bulk pork
   breakfast sausage
1 to 2 cups (4 to 8 ounces) shredded
   sharp Cheddar cheese

4 eggs
1 cup light cream
1/4 cup chopped green bell pepper
1/4 cup chopped red bell pepper
2 to 3 tablespoons chopped onion

Bake the pie shells using the package directions for about 5 minutes. Cool on a wire rack. Brown the sausage in a skillet, stirring until crumbly; drain. Combine the sausage and cheese in a bowl and mix well. Sprinkle over the bottom of the pie shells.

Lightly beat the eggs in a bowl. Combine the cream, bell peppers and onion in a bowl and mix well. Mix in the cream mixture and pour over the prepared layers. Bake in a preheated 375-degree oven for 30 to 35 minutes or until set. Cool on a wire rack for 10 minutes before serving.

Makes 2 pies

Breakfast Spice Bread

2 cups self-rising flour
2 cups sugar
1 teaspoon cinnamon
1 teaspoon ground allspice
1 teaspoon (scant) nutmeg

4 (2-ounce) jars baby food prunes
1/2 cup vegetable oil
3 eggs, lightly beaten
1/2 to 1 cup walnuts or
   pecans, chopped

Combine the self-rising flour, sugar, cinnamon, allspice and nutmeg in a bowl and mix well. Stir in the prunes, oil and eggs. Fold in the walnuts; do not overmix.

Spoon the batter into a greased bundt pan. Bake in a preheated 350-degree oven for 1 hour. Cool in the pan for 10 minutes. Invert onto a wire rack.

Makes 16 slices

Sour Cream Corn Bread

6 eggs

2 (15-ounce) cans cream-style corn

3 (8-ounce) packages corn bread mix

1 cup vegetable oil

2 teaspoons salt

2 cups sour cream

Whisk the eggs in a bowl until blended. Stir in the corn, corn bread mix, oil and salt. Fold in the sour cream until completely combined. Spread the batter in a greased 9×13-inch baking pan. Bake in a preheated 350-degree oven for 30 to 40 minutes or until light brown. Let stand for 5 minutes before slicing.

A favorite menu item served at Faculty and Staff Appreciation Luncheons.

Makes 2 dozen small squares

This corn bread bakes up beautifully. It is very moist, not crumbly, and slices easily. Delicious with chili.

Cheddar Muffins

3 cups all-purpose flour

4 1/2 teaspoons baking powder

1 1/2 teaspoons salt

6 tablespoons butter, chilled and cut into small pieces

12 ounces extra-sharp Cheddar cheese, coarsely shredded

1 1/2 cups milk

Mix the flour, baking powder and salt in a bowl. Cut in the butter until crumbly. Add the cheese and milk and stir until a sticky dough forms. At this point the dough may be stored, covered, in the refrigerator. Bring to room temperature before proceeding with the recipe.

Fill muffin cups sprayed with nonstick cooking spray three-fourths full. Bake in a preheated 425-degree oven on the middle oven rack for 15 to 20 minutes or until light brown. Remove the muffins to a wire rack to cool. Best served warm. Freeze for future use if desired.

Makes 12 to 16 muffins

Best-Ever White Bread

2 cups milk
2 tablespoons sugar
1 tablespoon lard or shortening
2 teaspoons salt
1 envelope dry yeast
1/4 cup warm (110- to 115-degree) water
6 1/2 cups (or more) all-purpose flour, sifted

Scald the milk in a saucepan. Stir in the sugar, lard and salt and let cool to lukewarm. Sprinkle the yeast over the warm water in a bowl and stir until dissolved.

Combine the milk mixture, dissolved yeast and 3 cups of the flour in a bowl and beat with a spoon until a smooth dough forms. Or, beat in a mixing bowl with an electric mixer at medium speed for 2 minutes or until smooth. Add the remaining 3 1/2 cups flour and mix until blended.

Knead the dough on a lightly floured surface for 8 to 10 minutes or until smooth and elastic. Shape the dough into a ball and place in a lightly greased bowl, turning to coat the surface. Let rise, covered, in a warm place (such as the oven with the light on) until doubled in bulk. Punch the dough down. Let rise, covered, for 45 minutes or until almost doubled in bulk.

Divide the dough into two equal portions. Shape each portion into a loaf in a 5x9-inch loaf pan. Let rise, covered, for 1 hour. Bake in a preheated 400-degree oven for 35 minutes or until golden brown. Cool in the pans for 10 minutes. Remove to a wire rack away from drafts to cool completely.

Makes 2 loaves

*T*his bread is very easy to prepare and lends itself to many variations. For special holidays, food coloring can be added, such as green for St. Patrick's Day and pastels for Easter. Add cinnamon and raisins for variety. For Whole Wheat Bread, use half all-purpose flour and half whole wheat flour. Originally published in *Raving Recipes*.

Chili Cheese Mexican Dip

8 ounces bulk pork breakfast sausage
   or ground beef
8 ounces cream cheese, softened
1/2 cup salsa
1/2 cup (2 ounces) shredded
   Cheddar cheese
1 (16-ounce) can chili beans

1/2 cup (2 ounces) shredded
   Cheddar cheese
2 to 3 tablespoons chopped canned
   jalapeño chiles
3 tablespoons sliced green onions
2 tablespoons sliced black olives
   (optional)

Brown the sausage in a skillet, stirring until crumbly; drain. Mix the cream cheese and salsa in a bowl. Spread over the bottom of a greased 9-inch baking dish. Sprinkle with the sausage and 1/2 cup Cheddar cheese. Top with the beans and sprinkle with 1/2 cup Cheddar cheese, the jalapeño chiles, green onions and olives. Bake in a preheated 350-degree oven for 15 to 20 minutes or until the cheese melts and the dip is heated through. Serve warm with tortilla chips.

Serves 6

Lentil Pâté

1 cup red lentils, rinsed and drained
2 1/2 cups water
1 cup bulgur or cracked wheat, rinsed
   and drained
1 large onion, chopped
1/2 cup olive oil

1/4 cup lemon juice
2 tablespoons cumin
1 tablespoon tomato paste
1 teaspoon salt
1/2 cup parsley, chopped

Combine the lentils and water in a saucepan. Cook over low heat until a small amount of water remains. Stir in the bulgur. Cook until all the water is absorbed, stirring frequently. This process will take about 45 minutes. Remove from the heat and cover.

Sauté the onion in the olive oil in a saucepan over medium-high heat until tender. Stir in the lemon juice, cumin, tomato paste and salt. Add the lentil mixture and mix well. Cook over low heat for 8 to 10 minutes or until the mixture begins to pull away from the side of the pan and is a doughy consistency. Remove from the heat and let stand, covered, for 1 hour. Stir in the parsley. Shape into a long narrow loaf. Chill, covered, in the refrigerator. Arrange the loaf on a platter lined with mixed salad greens. Serve with pita chips and/or assorted party crackers.

Makes 3 cups

Swiss Almond Spread

8 ounces light cream cheese, softened
1 1/2 cups (6 ounces) shredded Swiss cheese
1/2 cup Miracle Whip (do not substitute)
1/3 cup sliced almonds, toasted
2 tablespoons chopped green onions
Paprika to taste
2 tablespoons sliced almonds, toasted

Combine the cream cheese, Swiss cheese, Miracle Whip, 1/3 cup almonds and the green onions in a bowl and mix well. Spread in a 9-inch baking dish or quiche dish. Bake in a preheated 350-degree oven for 6 minutes. Remove from the oven and stir. Maintain the oven temperature.

Sprinkle paprika and 2 tablespoons almonds over the baked layer. Bake for 6 minutes longer or until hot and bubbly. Garnish with sliced green onions. Serve with vegetables, pita chips and/or assorted party crackers.

The flavor is enhanced if a high-quality Swiss cheese is used.

Makes 2 1/2 cups

Pigs in Cashmere Blankets

5 links sweet or hot Italian sausage
   (about 1 1/4 pounds)
1/2 cup peach preserves
1/4 cup hot mustard
1 tablespoon honey
1 sheet puff pastry, thawed

Grill the sausage over hot coals or sauté in a skillet until cooked through; drain. Let stand until cool. Mix the preserves, mustard and honey in a bowl until of a sauce consistency.

Roll the puff pastry into a 10×10-inch square on a lightly floured surface; make sure the fold seams are smooth. Cut into thirty 1 1/2×4-inch strips. Slice each sausage link lengthwise into halves and then into 2-inch chunks.

Spread some of the mustard sauce on each pastry strip. Place one chunk of sausage on each strip and enclose the sausage with the pastry, sealing the edges on the bottom. Arrange seam side down on a baking sheet lined with baking parchment. Chill for 30 to 60 minutes.

Bake in a preheated 400-degree oven for 15 to 20 minutes or until the pastry is puffed and golden brown. Serve warm with the remaining mustard sauce.

Makes 30

Spicy Won Tons

1 (16-ounce) package won ton wrappers
1 pound hot or mild bulk pork sausage
2 cups (8 ounces) shredded pepper jack cheese
2 cups (8 ounces) shredded Cheddar cheese
3/4 cup ranch salad dressing
1/3 cup finely chopped pimento-stuffed green olives
1/4 cup finely sliced green onions
1/3 cup finely chopped red bell pepper
1 jalapeño chile, seeded and minced

Lightly spray twenty-four miniature muffin cups with nonstick cooking spray. Separate the won ton wrappers. Fit the wrappers into the muffin cups and pleat the edges. Lightly spray with nonstick cooking spray. Bake in a preheated 350-degree oven for 8 to 9 minutes; do not allow the edges to overbrown. Maintain the oven temperature.

Brown the sausage in a skillet until crumbly. Drain on paper towels. Combine the sausage, cheese, salad dressing, olives, green onions, bell pepper and jalapeño chile in a bowl and mix well. Spoon evenly into each won ton cup. Bake for 9 to 10 minutes or until heated through. Serve warm.

The won tons can be prepared up to one day in advance. Store the won tons after the first baking in an airtight container at room temperature. Prepare the sausage filling one to two days in advance and store, covered, in the refrigerator. Reheat the filling in the microwave to room temperature before proceeding with the recipe.

Makes 2 dozen won tons

Red and White Chicken Chili

6 boneless skinless chicken breasts
2 tablespoons vegetable oil
$^1/_2$ teaspoon salt
1 onion, chopped
1 green bell pepper, chopped
2 garlic cloves, minced
2 (14-ounce) cans stewed tomatoes
1 (15-ounce) can pinto beans, drained and rinsed
$^2/_3$ cup picante sauce
1 teaspoon chili powder
1 teaspoon cumin

Slice the chicken breasts crosswise into halves and then cut into strips. Cut the strips into bite-size pieces. Heat 1 tablespoon of the oil in a Dutch oven over medium-high heat. Add the chicken and sprinkle with the salt. Sear until the chicken is cooked through, stirring frequently. Remove the chicken and all the pan drippings to a bowl.

Heat the remaining 1 tablespoon oil in the Dutch oven over medium heat. Add the onion, bell pepper and garlic and sauté until the onion is tender. Chop the tomatoes. Add the tomatoes with juice, beans, picante sauce, chili powder and cumin to the onion mixture and mix well. Stir in the chicken and pan drippings.

Simmer, covered, over low heat for 20 minutes. Taste and adjust the seasonings. Ladle into chili bowls and serve with shredded Cheddar cheese, sour cream, chopped scallions and/or chopped avocado. Dial up the heat by adding hot sauce, if desired.

Serves 10

Quick and easy enough to whip up on a school night.

Red Hot Chili for a Crowd

1 pound ground beef
1 pound ground turkey
1 pound ground pork
3 pounds beef round, cut into chunks
1 large onion, chopped
1 large green bell pepper, chopped
1 large red bell pepper, chopped
1 or 2 jalapeño chiles, chopped
1 (28-ounce) can crushed tomatoes
2 or 3 (12-ounce) cans beer
1/4 cup chili powder
1/4 cup cumin
1 teaspoon paprika
1/4 to 1/2 teaspoon cayenne pepper (optional)
Salt and black pepper to taste
2 (15-ounce) cans beans, drained and rinsed
    (red kidney, pinto, black, etc.)

Brown the ground beef, ground turkey and ground pork in a large Dutch oven, stirring until crumbly; drain. Add the beef round, onion, bell peppers and jalapeño chile and mix well. Stir in the tomatoes, beer, chili powder, cumin, paprika, cayenne pepper, salt and black pepper.

Simmer for 4 hours or until the beef round is tender, stirring occasionally. Add the beans and simmer for 30 to 60 minutes longer, adding additional beer as needed for the desired consistency. Taste and adjust the seasonings. Ladle into chili bowls.

Serves 10 to 12

This is a real man friendly chili … tons and tons of meat and just enough beans.

Sausage and Corn Chowder

1 pound mild or hot bulk pork sausage	1 teaspoon salt
1 small onion, chopped	1 teaspoon basil
4 cups coarsely chopped Yukon gold potatoes	1/8 teaspoon pepper
	1 (14-ounce) can cream-style corn
2 cups water	1 (15-ounce) can whole kernel corn
1 tablespoon parsley	1 1/2 cups half-and-half

Brown the sausage with the onion in a skillet, stirring until the sausage is crumbly and the onion is tender; drain. Combine the potatoes, water, parsley, salt, basil and pepper in a stockpot. Cook for 15 minutes or until the potatoes are tender.

Add the sausage mixture, corn and half-and-half and mix well. Cook for 5 to 10 minutes longer or until heated through. Ladle into soup bowls and serve immediately.

Serves 6

Swiss Potato Soup

12 slices bacon, coarsely chopped	6 cups chicken stock or chicken broth
1 (1-pound) head cabbage, coarsely chopped	2 cups (8 ounces) shredded Gruyère cheese
1 onion, coarsely chopped	1 cup light cream
2 leeks, or 4 scallions, coarsely chopped	1 tablespoon dill weed
4 potatoes, peeled and chopped	Salt and pepper to taste

Sauté the bacon in a stockpot for 3 minutes. Add the cabbage, onion and leeks and sauté for 5 minutes longer. Stir in the potatoes and stock. Bring to a boil and then reduce the heat.

Simmer for 40 minutes, stirring occasionally. Gradually add the cheese and cook over medium heat until the cheese melts, stirring constantly; do not boil. Just before serving, mix in the cream and dill weed and season with salt and pepper. Simmer just until heated through; do not boil. Ladle into soup bowls.

Serves 10 to 12

Roasted Tomato Soup

3 pounds plum tomatoes, cored and
    cut into halves
8 sprigs of thyme
4 garlic cloves, minced
Kosher salt and freshly ground
    pepper to taste
3 tablespoons olive oil
1/2 cup mascarpone cheese
1/2 cup (2 ounces) grated
    Parmigiano-Reggiano cheese
2 tablespoons olive oil
1 yellow onion, chopped
3 cups chicken stock
4 slices country-style bread, toasted
    and broken

Arrange the tomato halves cut sides up on a baking sheet. Remove the leaves from the thyme sprigs and scatter the leaves over the tomatoes. Sprinkle with the garlic, salt and pepper. Drizzle with 3 tablespoons olive oil. Roast in a preheated 275 degreee oven for 2 hours or until the tomatoes are slightly dry and some of the skins have burst. Remove and discard the tomato skins.

Mix the mascarpone cheese and Parmigiano-Reggiano cheese in a bowl using a rubber spatula until smooth. Chill, covered, in the refrigerator. Pass the tomatoes through a tomato press or through a fine strainer into a bowl, discarding the solids.

Heat 2 tablespoons olive oil in a large saucepan over medium heat. Add the onion and sauté for 4 to 6 minutes or until tender. Stir in the puréed tomatoes, stock and bread and simmer for 5 minutes. Process the soup in a blender until puréed and season with salt and pepper. Ladle the soup into heated soup bowls and top each with a dollop of the mascarpone cheese mixture. Serve immediately.

Serves 6

Crunchy Orange Almond Salad

Orange Dressing
1/4 cup orange juice
3 1/2 tablespoons olive oil
2 tablespoons rice wine vinegar
1 teaspoon sugar
Salt and pepper to taste

Salad
1/2 cup slivered almonds
3 tablespoons sugar
3 cups bite-size pieces romaine
3 cups mixed baby salad greens
1 (15-ounce) can mandarin
  oranges, drained
1/2 cup chopped celery
1/2 cup rice noodles

To prepare the dressing, whisk the orange juice, olive oil, vinegar and sugar in a bowl until combined. Season with salt and pepper.

To prepare the salad, combine the almonds and sugar in a small skillet. Cook over medium-low heat until the sugar melts and coats the almonds. Remove the almonds to a plate to cool. Toss the romaine, salad greens, mandarin oranges and celery in a salad bowl. Add the dressing and mix well. Sprinkle with the almonds and noodles.

Serves 6

*M*akes a great main dish salad with the addition of grilled chicken.

Blue Cheese Coleslaw

1 cup light mayonnaise
1/4 cup Dijon mustard
2 tablespoons sugar

2 tablespoons cider vinegar
16 ounces shredded coleslaw mix
1/3 cup crumbled blue cheese

Whisk the mayonnaise, Dijon mustard, sugar and vinegar in a bowl until blended. Add the coleslaw mix and blue cheese and stir to coat. Chill, covered, until serving time.

Serves 6 to 8

*T*his coleslaw pairs well with the North Carolina Barbecue on page 116.

Burgundy Beef Tips

1/2 cup all-purpose flour
1/2 onion, chopped
1/2 cup herb-seasoned stuffing mix
2 pounds sirloin beef cubes
2 (10-ounce) cans beef consommé

1/2 teaspoon salt
1/2 teaspoon pepper
1 cup sherry
Hot cooked white rice, wild rice
    or noodles

Combine the flour, onion and stuffing mix in a large Dutch oven and mix well. Stir in the beef cubes, consommé, salt and pepper. Gently stir in the sherry.

Bake, uncovered, in a preheated 300-degree oven for 3 hours. Serve over hot cooked white rice, wild rice or noodles. Garnish with chopped flat-leaf parsley.

Goes great with a simple green salad.

Serves 6

Beef Bourguignon

3 onions, sliced
2 tablespoons (or more)
    bacon drippings
2 pounds lean beef stew meat
2 tablespoons all-purpose flour
1/4 teaspoon salt
1/4 teaspoon pepper

1/4 teaspoon marjoram
1/4 teaspoon thyme
1 cup beef bouillon
1 cup dry red wine
8 to 16 ounces mushrooms, sliced
12 small new potatoes (optional)

Cook the onions in the bacon drippings in a large Dutch oven until brown. Remove the onions to a platter using a slotted spoon, reserving the pan drippings. Cut the stew meat into 1-inch pieces and add to the reserved pan drippings. Cook until brown on all sides, adding additional bacon drippings if needed. Sprinkle the flour, salt, pepper, marjoram and thyme over the stew meat. Add the bouillon and wine and lightly stir.

Simmer, covered, over the lowest possible heat for 1 to 1 1/2 hours. Add the onions, mushrooms and potatoes and cook for 30 to 45 minutes or until the vegetables are tender, stirring occasionally.

Serves 6

Citrus-Marinated Pork Tenderloin

3/4 cup orange juice
1/2 cup chopped onion
1/4 cup lime juice
1/4 cup cilantro
2 garlic cloves, chopped
1 tablespoon oregano
1/2 teaspoon cumin
1/2 teaspoon orange zest (optional)
1/2 teaspoon lime zest
1/2 cup olive oil
Salt and pepper to taste
2 (1- to 1 1/4-pound) pork tenderloins
1 tablespoon vegetable oil

Combine the orange juice, onion, lime juice, cilantro, garlic, oregano, cumin, orange zest and lime zest in a blender. Process until puréed. Add the olive oil and process until combined. Season with salt and pepper. Reserve 1/2 cup of the marinade and chill. Pour the remaining marinade over the tenderloins in a glass dish, turning to coat.

Marinate, covered, in the refrigerator for 8 to 10 hours, turning occasionally. Remove the tenderloins from the marinade and pat dry with paper towels, discarding the used marinade. Heat the vegetable oil in a large ovenproof skillet over high heat. Sear the tenderloins on all sides until brown.

Roast in a preheated 375-degree oven for 20 to 30 minutes or to the desired degree of doneness. Simmer the reserved 1/2 cup marinade in a saucepan for 20 minutes. Let the tenderloins stand for 5 to 10 minutes and slice as desired. Serve with the warm marinade.

Grill the tenderloins if desired.

Serves 6 to 8

Herb-Roasted Loin of Pork

1 teaspoon salt
1/2 teaspoon paprika
1/2 teaspoon dry mustard
1/2 teaspoon thyme
1/2 teaspoon lemon pepper

1 shallot, minced
2 to 3 teaspoons olive oil
1 (2-pound) pork loin roast
1/4 cup all-purpose flour

Mix the salt, paprika, dry mustard, thyme, lemon pepper and shallot in a bowl. Add enough of the olive oil to make a loose paste. Rub over the surface of the roast and coat with the flour, shaking the roast to remove any excess flour. Let stand until room temperature.

Arrange the roast fat side up on a greased rack in a shallow roasting pan. Place in a preheated 450-degree oven. Reduce the oven temperature to 350 degrees and roast for 1 hour and 10 minutes or until a meat thermometer registers 160 degrees for medium. Let stand, covered with foil, for 10 minutes before slicing.

Serves 4

North Carolina Barbecue

1 (3- to 5-pound) boneless pork
    sirloin roast
2 cups cider vinegar
1/2 cup packed dark brown sugar
1/4 cup extra-virgin olive oil

3 tablespoons crushed red
    pepper flakes
4 teaspoons salt
2 teaspoons black pepper

Trim any excess fat from the pork and place the pork in a slow cooker. Cook on High for 6 hours. Do not add any ingredients to the slow cooker as the pork will form its own broth. Whisk the vinegar, brown sugar, olive oil, red pepper flakes, salt and black pepper in a saucepan until combined and bring to a low boil. Remove from the heat and let stand on the stovetop for 2 to 3 hours. Remove the pork to a platter, reserving the juices. Shred the pork with a knife and fork and return the shredded pork to the reserved juices. Add the vinegar sauce and mix to coat.

Serves 8

Pairs nicely with the Blue Cheese Coleslaw on page 113.

Blackened Chicken Cordon Bleu

6 boneless skinless chicken breasts
2 tablespoons Creole seasoning
3 tablespoons butter
3/4 cup chopped tasso, prosciutto or
    Canadian bacon
1 cup sliced mushrooms
1/4 cup sliced green onions
2 teaspoons pepper
1 1/2 cups heavy cream
3/4 cup (3 ounces) freshly grated
    Parmesan cheese
6 cups hot cooked rice
1/4 cup (1 ounce) freshly grated
    Parmesan cheese

Dust the chicken with the Creole seasoning. Melt the butter in a large skillet over high heat. Add the chicken and cook for 3 minutes. Turn and cook for 2 minutes on the remaining side to blacken. Remove the chicken to a baking pan, reserving the pan drippings. Bake in a preheated 350-degree oven for 10 to 20 minutes or until the chicken is cooked through.

Stir the tasso, mushrooms, green onions and pepper into the reserved pan drippings. Cook over medium heat until the mushrooms are tender. Add the cream and cook until the sauce is slightly thickened. Stir in 3/4 cup cheese.

Spoon 1 cup of the rice on each of six serving plates. Top each serving with one chicken breast and an equal portion of the tasso sauce. Sprinkle evenly with 1/4 cup cheese. Serve immediately.

May also serve over mashed potatoes.

Serves 6

Chicken Caprese with Tomato Basil Sauce

3 tablespoons olive oil
2 tablespoons lemon juice
2/3 cup soft bread crumbs
1/3 cup crumbled feta cheese
1 tablespoon chopped fresh basil, or
    1 teaspoon dried basil
1/4 teaspoon salt
1/4 teaspoon pepper
4 boneless skinless chicken breasts
1 cup spaghetti sauce
2 tablespoons whipping cream or light sour cream
1 tablespoon chopped fresh basil, or
    1 teaspoon dried basil

Whisk the olive oil and lemon juice in a bowl until blended. Mix the bread crumbs, cheese, 1 tablespoon basil, the salt and pepper in a shallow dish. Dip the chicken in the lemon juice mixture and coat with the bread crumb mixture, pressing to adhere.

Arrange the chicken in a single layer in a lightly greased baking dish. Bake in a preheated 375-degree oven for 30 minutes or until the chicken is cooked through and light brown.

Combine the spaghetti sauce, cream and 1 tablespoon basil in a saucepan and mix well. Cook over low heat for 5 minutes or until heated through, stirring occasionally. Spoon the sauce evenly on each of four serving plates and arrange one chicken breast on each plate, or drizzle the sauce over the top of each chicken breast. Garnish with sprigs of basil and serve immediately.

Serves 4

Pan-Seared Sea Scallops in Champagne Cream Sauce

1 1/2 pounds large sea scallops
Salt and pepper to taste
1 tablespoon unsalted butter
1 tablespoon extra-virgin olive oil
1/2 cup Champagne or white wine
1/2 cup whipping cream

Pat the scallops dry with paper towels and season with salt and pepper. Heat the butter and olive oil in a large skillet over high heat until the butter melts. Add the scallops and cook for 2 to 3 minutes or until golden brown on one side. Turn the scallops and cook until golden brown on the remaining side. Remove the scallops to a platter, reserving the pan drippings.

Heat the Champagne with the reserved pan drippings until reduced by half, stirring to release any browned bits from the bottom of the skillet. Reduce the heat to low and stir in the cream. Add the scallops and simmer just until heated through.

Serves 4

Serve with White Corn Risotto on page 125 and steamed green beans. For a nice presentation, mound equal portions of the risotto in the center of each of four serving plates and arrange three scallops over the top of each risotto serving. Drizzle with the Champagne cream sauce.

Shrimp and Grits Casserole

Shrimp and Sauce

1 tablespoon kosher salt or sea salt
2 cups cold water
1 cup ice cubes
1 1/2 pounds large shrimp, peeled
    and deveined
2 to 3 tablespoons (or more) olive oil
1 or 2 garlic cloves, minced
4 to 6 green onions, chopped
Dash of Greek seasoning
2/3 cup chicken broth
1 tablespoon cornstarch

Cheese Grits

2 cups chicken stock
2/3 cup milk
2/3 cup quick-cooking grits
1 cup (4 ounces) shredded
    Cheddar cheese
2 tablespoons butter
1/4 teaspoon salt
1/4 teaspoon hot red pepper sauce
2 eggs, beaten

To prepare the shrimp, dissolve the salt in the cold water in a large bowl. Stir in the ice cubes and shrimp. Let the shrimp soak in the brine mixture in the refrigerator for 30 minutes. Drain and rinse the shrimp. Pat dry with paper towels. Heat 2 tablespoons of the olive oil in a large sauté pan over medium-high heat until very hot but not smoking. Sear the shrimp in batches in the hot oil by placing them one-by-one without crowding in the skillet, turning the first shrimp to the opposite side about as soon as the last shrimp has been added to the skillet. Once both sides have been seared, remove the shrimp to a large bowl. The shrimp will not be cooked through. Repeat this process until all of the shrimp have been seared, adding olive oil as needed and reserving the pan drippings. Cool the pan drippings slightly. Sauté the garlic, green onions and Greek seasoning in the reserved pan drippings for 1 minute, adding olive oil if needed. Add to the shrimp and mix well. Whisk 1/3 cup of the broth and the cornstarch in a bowl until blended. Add the remaining 1/3 cup broth to the sauté pan used to sear the shrimp. Heat over medium heat, scraping the bottom to dislodge any browned bits. Add the cornstarch mixture and cook until thickened. Stir the sauce into the shrimp mixture.

To prepare the grits, bring the stock and milk to a boil in a saucepan. Stir in the grits and cook for 4 to 5 minutes or until thickened, stirring occasionally. Remove from the heat and stir in cheese, butter, salt and hot sauce. Mix in the eggs and cook until thickened, stirring frequently. Stir in the shrimp mixture and spoon into a greased 8×11-inch baking dish. Bake in a preheated 350-degree oven for 30 to 40 minutes or until heated through.

You may prepare up to one day in advance and store, covered, in the refrigerator. Bring to room temperature before baking.

Serves 6

Linguini with Sun-Dried Tomatoes and Olives

1 pound fresh or dried linguini
Salt to taste
1 to 2 tablespoons olive oil
2 garlic cloves, thinly sliced
1 cup thinly sliced sun-dried tomatoes
1 cup sliced pitted kalamata olives
1 1/2 cups chicken broth
1 1/2 cups heavy cream
1/2 cup white wine
Freshly ground pepper to taste
1 cup fresh basil leaves, julienned
1/2 cup chopped green onions
Freshly grated Parmesan cheese to taste
3 boneless skinless chicken breasts, grilled and
    cut into strips (optional)

Cook the pasta in boiling salted water in a saucepan using the package directions; drain. Cover to keep warm. Heat the olive oil in a large saucepan over medium-high heat. Sauté the garlic in the hot oil for 1 minute or just until it begins to turn golden brown. Stir in the tomatoes and olives and sauté for 1 minute longer. Mix in the broth, cream and wine and bring to a simmer.

Simmer for 12 to 15 minutes or until the sauce is thick enough to coat the back of a spoon. Season with salt and pepper. Reduce the heat to low and stir in the basil and green onions. Cook for 1 minute. Pour the sauce over the pasta in a bowl and toss to combine. Sprinkle with cheese and top with the chicken strips. Serve immediately.

Serves 3 to 4

Pasta Shells with Mushrooms and Radicchio

6 tablespoons unsalted butter
12 ounces shiitake mushrooms,
    stems removed and mushrooms sliced
Pinch of kosher salt
16 ounces medium pasta shells
2¹/2 cups heavy cream
1 cup (4 ounces) freshly grated
    Parmesan cheese
1 cup (4 ounces) shredded fontina cheese
1/2 cup crumbled Gorgonzola cheese
1 small head radicchio, shredded
6 fresh sage leaves, shredded
2 tablespoons unsalted butter

Melt 6 tablespoons butter in a sauté pan over medium heat and add the mushrooms. Sauté for 5 minutes and season with the salt. Bring a large saucepan of water to a boil and add the pasta. Cook for 10 minutes or until al dente. Drain, but do not rinse.

Combine the mushrooms, cream, Parmesan cheese, fontina cheese, Gorgonzola cheese, radicchio and sage in a large bowl and mix well. Add the pasta and toss to combine. Spoon into a buttered baking dish and dot with 2 tablespoons butter. Bake in a preheated 450-degree oven for 30 minutes or until light brown and bubbly.

This pasta dish may be prepared in advance and stored, covered, in the refrigerator until just before baking. Wonderful paired with beef tenderloin or pork tenderloin, but it is also satisfying enough to serve as a main entrée. Reheat any leftovers in the oven to prevent the cheese from separating.

Serves 6 to 8 as a side dish

Hoppin' John

1 cup dried black-eyed peas
1 onion, cut into quarters
2 ribs celery, chopped
2 garlic cloves
1/2 fresh jalapeño chile
3 ounces kielbasa, cut into small chunks
2 cups chicken broth
1 bay leaf
Salt and pepper to taste

Sort and rinse the peas and place in a 2-quart saucepan. Add enough water to cover the peas by 2 inches. Bring to a boil and boil for 2 minutes. Remove from the heat and let stand for 1 hour; drain. Process the onion, celery, garlic and jalapeño chile in a food processor until coarsely chopped.

Combine the peas, onion mixture, kielbasa, broth, bay leaf, salt and pepper in a 2-quart saucepan. Bring to a boil and then reduce the heat. Simmer for 20 to 30 minutes or until the peas are tender but not falling apart. Discard the bay leaf. Serve with hot cooked rice.

Makes 4 entrée servings, or 6 side dish servings

For Vegetarian Hoppin' John, omit the kielbasa and substitute water for the chicken broth. Add vegetable seasonings or fresh herbs such as coriander or cilantro. Season with salt and pepper.

Sautéed Collard Greens

1 bunch collard greens (about 1 1/2 pounds)
3 tablespoons olive oil
2 garlic cloves, crushed
1 shallot, minced
1/2 cup chicken broth
Salt and pepper to taste

Remove and discard any yellow, limp or bruised leaves from the collards. Discard the tough central stems of the remaining leaves. Rinse the collards several times in a sink full of cold water to remove any grit. Shake the excess water from the collards and dry on paper towels.

Heat the olive oil in a large skillet. Add the garlic and shallot and sauté over medium heat for 1 to 2 minutes or until the shallot just begins to turn translucent. Tear the collards into fairly large pieces and add to the skillet. Reduce the heat to low.

Cook for about 10 minutes, stirring almost constantly until the collards are wilted but still bright green. Add the broth and continue to cook over low heat for about 10 minutes longer or until most of the broth has been absorbed. Season with salt and pepper.

Serves 4

Fresh baby spinach is readily available rinsed and ready to eat. Try wilting it in some sesame oil for a quick-and-easy side dish.

White Corn Risotto

1 tablespoon unsalted butter
1 cup frozen white Shoe Peg corn
Salt and pepper to taste
2 tablespoons unsalted butter
1 tablespoon olive oil
2 shallots, minced
1 cup arborio rice
1 cup dry white wine
1 quart (4 cups) organic chicken broth, simmering
1/2 cup (2 ounces) grated Parmesan cheese
1 tablespoon unsalted butter

Melt 1 tablespoon butter in a skillet over medium heat. Stir in the corn, salt and pepper. Sauté until the corn is light brown.

Melt 2 tablespoons butter with the olive oil in a large heavy saucepan over medium heat. Add the shallots and sauté until tender. Add the rice and stir until coated. Stir in the wine.

Simmer until all of the liquid is absorbed. Add the warm broth 1 to 2 ladlefuls at a time and simmer until all of the broth is absorbed, stirring occasionally. Continue adding the broth 1 to 2 ladlefuls at a time and simmering until the broth is absorbed and the rice is creamy and tender, stirring occasionally. Stir in the corn with the last ladleful of broth. Add the cheese and 1 tablespoon butter and mix well. Season with salt and pepper and serve.

Serve as a side dish to roasted chicken or Pan-Seared Sea Scallops in Champagne Cream Sauce on page 119.

Serves 4

*H*ate Brussels sprouts? Try shredding them like you would cabbage. Sauté them in some olive oil until tender-crisp and beginning to caramelize. Season with salt and pepper. You will change your mind.

Frosted Fudge Brownies

Brownies
2 cups sugar
1 1/2 cups all-purpose flour
1 teaspoon salt
1 teaspoon baking soda
1 cup (2 sticks) margarine (do not use butter)
4 ounces unsweetened chocolate
4 eggs, lightly beaten
1 teaspoon vanilla extract
1 cup chopped pecans (optional)

Chocolate Icing
1/2 cup (1 stick) margarine
2 ounces unsweetened chocolate
1 (1-pound) package confectioners' sugar
1/2 to 3/4 (5-ounce) can evaporated milk

To prepare the brownies, mix the sugar, flour, salt and baking soda together. Melt the margarine and chocolate in a saucepan over medium heat, stirring occasionally. Remove from the heat and stir in the sugar mixture. Add the eggs and vanilla and mix well. Stir in the pecans.

Spread the batter in a greased and floured 10×15-inch baking sheet with sides. (This size baking sheet must be used.) Bake in a preheated 325-degree oven for 25 to 30 minutes or until the brownies test done. Cool in the pan on a wire rack.

To prepare the icing, melt the margarine with the chocolate in a saucepan over medium heat, stirring occasionally. Remove from the heat and add the confectioners' sugar and 1/2 of the evaporated milk. Stir until of a spreading consistency, adding additional evaporated milk as needed. Spread the hot icing over the cooled brownies. Let stand until cool and set. Cut into squares. Store in an airtight container.

Makes 4 dozen brownies

Butterscotch Pie

Pie
3/4 cup packed brown sugar
1/3 cup all-purpose flour
1/4 teaspoon salt
2 cups milk
3 egg yolks, lightly beaten
3 tablespoons butter
1 teaspoon vanilla extract
1 baked (9-inch) pie shell

Meringue
3 egg whites
1/2 teaspoon vanilla extract
1/4 teaspoon cream of tartar
6 tablespoons sugar

To prepare the pie, combine the brown sugar, flour and salt in a saucepan and mix well. Add the milk gradually, stirring until combined. Cook over medium-high heat until bubbly, stirring constantly. Cook for 2 minutes longer, stirring constantly. Remove from the heat.

Gradually stir a moderate amount of the hot mixture into the egg yolks. Add the egg yolks back to the hot mixture and mix until blended. Cook for 2 minutes, stirring constantly. Remove from the heat and stir in the butter and vanilla. Spread the filling in the pie shell.

To prepare the meringue, beat the egg whites, vanilla and cream of tartar in a mixing bowl until soft peaks form. Add the sugar gradually, beating constantly until stiff, glossy peaks form and the sugar dissolves.

Spread the meringue over the warm pie filling, sealing to the edge. Bake in a preheated 350-degree oven for 12 to 15 minutes or until the meringue is golden brown. Let stand until cool.

Serves 6 to 8

Mixed Berry Pie with Pecan-Orange Lattice Crust

Crust

1/2 cup pecans, toasted
2 1/4 cups all-purpose flour
1/2 cup sugar
1 tablespoon grated orange zest
3/4 teaspoon salt
3/4 cup (1 1/2 sticks) unsalted butter,
    chilled and cut into 1/2-inch pieces
5 tablespoons (about) ice water

Berry Filling

1 1/3 cups sugar

1/4 cup orange marmalade
1/4 cup cornstarch
1 tablespoon grated orange zest
1/4 teaspoon ground allspice
1 3/4 cups frozen unsweetened
    raspberries, thawed and drained
1 1/2 cups frozen unsweetened
    blueberries, thawed and drained
1 1/4 cups fresh or thawed
    frozen cranberries
1 egg, beaten
1 tablespoon sugar

To prepare the crust, process the pecans in a food processor until finely ground. Add the flour, sugar, orange zest and salt and process until blended. Add the butter and process until the mixture resembles coarse meal. Add the ice water by tablespoonfuls and pulse several times until moist clumps form. Shape the pastry into a ball and divide into two portions, one portion slightly larger than the other. Flatten the portions into disks and wrap each disk in plastic wrap. Chill for 1 hour. The pastry may be prepared up to 2 days in advance and stored in the refrigerator. Let the pastry stand at room temperature until slightly softened before proceeding with the recipe.

To prepare the filling, combine 1 1/3 cups sugar, the marmalade, cornstarch, orange zest and allspice in a large bowl and mix well. Add the raspberries, blueberries and cranberries and toss gently. Roll the larger pastry disk into a 13-inch round on a lightly floured surface. Fit the round into a 9-inch pie plate. Trim the overhang to 1 1/2 inches. Roll the remaining pastry disk into a 12-inch round on a lightly floured surface. Cut the round into fourteen 1/2-inch strips. Mound the berry filling in the prepared pie plate. Arrange seven dough strips evenly spaced over the filling. Form the lattice by placing the remaining pastry strips atop and at right angles to the first seven strips. Trim the ends of the strips even with the overhang of the bottom pastry. Fold the strip ends and overhang under, pressing to seal and forming a high-standing rim. Brush the lattice with the egg and sprinkle with 1 tablespoon sugar. Place the pie plate on a baking sheet lined with foil. Bake in a preheated 375-degree oven on a rack positioned in the bottom third of the oven for 1 hour and 15 minutes. Check the pie halfway through the baking process, covering the pastry rim with foil if needed to prevent overbrowning.

Serves 8

Cranberry Swirl Cheesecake

2 packages Pepperidge Farm Bordeaux cookies
1/4 cup (1/2 stick) butter, melted
1 (16-ounce) can whole cranberry sauce
2 teaspoons cinnamon
1/4 teaspoon ground cloves
24 ounces cream cheese, softened
1 cup sugar
1 tablespoon cornstarch
4 eggs
1 teaspoon vanilla extract

Crush enough of the cookies to measure 2 1/4 cups. Mix the cookie crumbs and butter in a bowl until crumbly. Pat over the bottom of a lightly greased 9-inch springform pan. Bake in a preheated 350-degree oven for 10 minutes. Let stand until cool. Maintain the oven temperature.

Process the cranberry sauce, cinnamon and cloves in a food processor or blender until smooth. Beat the cream cheese in a mixing bowl at medium speed until creamy. Add the sugar and cornstarch and beat until blended. Add the eggs one at a time, beating just until blended after each addition. Stir in the vanilla.

Spread one-half of the cream cheese mixture over the baked layer and spoon one-half of the cranberry mixture over the top. Swirl with a knife. Layer with the remaining cream cheese mixture and the remaining cranberry mixture and swirl with a knife. Bake for 15 minutes. Reduce the oven temperature to 225 degrees and bake for 1 hour and 10 minutes longer. Remove the cheesecake from the oven and run a sharp knife around the edge of the pan. Turn off the oven and return the cheesecake to the oven. Let stand with the door closed for 30 minutes. Store, covered, in the refrigerator.

Serves 10

Second Empire Sweet Potato Bread Pudding

2 loaves honey cornmeal bread or challah
    (preferably day old or less), torn into
    small pieces
5 cups heavy cream
1 3/4 cups packed brown sugar
1 1/4 cups milk
5 eggs
1 egg yolk
2 cups roasted sweet potato purée
1 1/2 to 2 cups raisins
1 1/2 to 2 cups dried cherries
1 tablespoon nutmeg, or to taste
1 teaspoon cinnamon, or to taste

Spread the bread pieces on a baking sheet. Heat in a preheated 350-degree oven until warm but not toasted. Maintain the oven temperature.

Bring the cream, brown sugar and milk to a boil in a saucepan. Whisk the eggs and egg yolk in a bowl until blended. Stir a small amount of the hot cream mixture into the eggs; stir the eggs into the hot mixture.

Pour the hot mixture over the bread pieces in a bowl and fold until the bread is saturated. Soak, covered, for 20 to 30 minutes and then stir. Add the sweet potato purée, raisins, cherries, nutmeg and cinnamon and mix well. Spoon into eight buttered ramekins. Bake for 25 to 30 minutes or until set.

Serves 8

Second Empire's talented executive chef, Daniel Schurr, honors North Carolina's state vegetable with a delectable, elegant dessert. It is an appropriate ending to any meal and is served there amid the grandeur of a Victorian mansion, creatively restored by the Reynolds family into an award-winning restaurant and tavern.

Pots de Crème

3/4 cup milk
1 cup (6 ounces) chocolate chips
2 tablespoons sugar
1 egg
Pinch of salt
1 teaspoon vanilla extract

Scald the milk in a saucepan. Combine the scalded milk, chocolate chips, sugar, egg, salt and vanilla in a blender. Process on medium speed for 1 minute.

Pour into four pot de crème cups and chill for several hours. Serve with whipped cream and fresh berries.

If you are concerned about using raw eggs, use eggs pasteurized in their shells, which are sold at some specialty food stores, or use an equivalent amount of pasteurized egg substitute.

Serves 4

This is a wonderfully easy dessert. It has a luscious chocolate flavor…no one can believe how simple it is to prepare. Originally published in *Raving Recipes*.

In the North Carolina Piedmont, unseasonably warm days in late winter sporadically tease the senses and cause flowers to burst forth in bloom long before winter officially gives way to spring. As spring approaches, those on campus seem to discover renewed energy from the warm, breezy skies that follow chilly mornings. Students enthusiastically welcome the opportunity to play outside sports again as well as prepare for end-of-the-year class plays, projects, and trips. At the Passover Chapel service, the Ravenscroft community celebrates this season of renewal and hope.

Throughout the spring season, you may find Ravenscroft students exploring the world—from field trips to the sandy shores or mountain peaks of our beautiful state, to excursions beyond, even across oceans to countries abroad. These travels serve to heighten their awareness of surrounding terrains and inspire their senses to gain new understandings of other cultures. While on these journeys, Ravenscroft students may contribute skills and energy to community service projects or share musical talents that help bridge gaps between cultures and across language divides.

Families do not have to venture far from campus to find fields of fresh strawberries, ripe for picking and sweetened naturally by spring rains and the continually warming Southern sun. After a fun afternoon of gathering these delicious jewels, enjoy Chocolate Strawberry Decadence to awaken your senses or savor Strawberries with Grand Marnier Sauce for a simple, but very elegant, ending to a spring luncheon. As warmer days coax you outside, prepare some Classic Southern Pimento Cheese, Curried Chicken Canapés, and Minted Fruit Salad and ask your neighbors to join you on the terrace for a light afternoon repast. The recipes that follow will take you from special meals for celebrating Easter or Passover to delightful preparations for family evenings and spring entertaining.

Spring
Break

Chapter Index

Bacon-Stuffed Deviled Eggs

Bacon and Egg Puff

Ham and Asparagus Quiche

Southern Biscuits

Quick Pecan Rolls

Cranberry Scones with
     Orange-Honey Butter

Curried Chicken Canapés

Artichoke Cheese Spread

Classic Southern Pimento Cheese

Chicken, Basil and Cashew Pâté

Buttery Ham Spread

Smoked Salmon Mousse with Caviar

Cheese Krispies

Minted Fruit Salad

Blueberry Gelatin Salad

Marinated Asparagus Salad

New Potato and Chive Salad

Warm Pancetta, Goat Cheese and
     Spinach Salad

Asian Chicken Salad with Peanut Dressing

Blue Cheese Bow Tie Pasta Salad

Bourbon-Marinated Beef Tenderloin

Beef and Scallion Bundles

Pineapple-Glazed Ham

Chicken and Asparagus Casserole

Cache Chicken

Chicken with Sun-Dried Tomato Sauce

Salmon with Tomatoes, Basil and
     White Beans

Barbecued Salmon with Cucumber Salsa

Crab Cakes

Baked Lemon Shrimp

Pasta Primavera

Roasted Green Beans

Onion Tart

Sweet Potato Soufflé

Couscous à la Grecque

Apricot Rice Pilaf

Kentucky Butter Cake

Chocolate Strawberry Decadence

French Cream Cake

White Chocolate Lemon Curd Layer Cake

Mexican Brownies

Mint Meringue Cookies

Oatmeal Lace Cookies

Angus Barn Key Lime Cheesecake

Strawberries with Grand Marnier Sauce

Raspberry Dessert Sauce

Menus

Sunday Brunch with Friends

Smoked Salmon Mousse with Caviar

Bacon and Egg Puff

Quick Pecan Rolls

Strawberries with Grand Marnier Sauce

Southern Easter Dinner

Bacon-Stuffed Deviled Eggs

Pineapple-Glazed Ham

Sweet Potato Soufflé

Marinated Asparagus Salad

Cranberry Scones with
    Orange-Honey Butter

White Chocolate Lemon Curd
    Layer Cake

Derby Day

Classic Southern Pimento Cheese

Bourbon-Marinated Beef Tenderloin

Blue Cheese Bow Tie Pasta Salad

Kentucky Butter Cake

*2006 Tobacco Road Cabernet Sauvignon
    "The Tradition," Napa Valley*

Mother's Day Luncheon

Cheese Krispies

Barbecued Salmon with Cucumber Salsa

New Potato and Chive Salad

Roasted Green Beans

Raspberry Dessert Sauce over
    Vanilla Ice Cream

Oatmeal Lace Cookies

Spring Garden Party

Chicken, Basil and Cashew Pâté

Ham and Asparagus Quiche

Minted Fruit Salad

Chocolate Strawberry Decadence

Bridal Shower

Curried Chicken Canapés

Buttery Ham Spread on
    Southern Biscuits

Blueberry Gelatin Salad

Mint Meringue Cookies

Bacon-Stuffed Deviled Eggs

6 slices bacon, crisp-cooked
6 hard-cooked eggs
1/4 cup mayonnaise
1 teaspoon spicy brown mustard
1/4 to 1/2 teaspoon paprika

Crumble and mince the bacon, reserving a few larger pieces for garnish. Cut the eggs lengthwise into halves. Remove the yolks to a bowl and reserve the whites.

Press the yolks through a sieve into a bowl, using the back of a spoon. Combine the yolks, minced bacon, mayonnaise, mustard and paprika in a bowl and stir until combined. Mound in the reserved egg whites and arrange on a serving platter. Chill, covered, for 1 hour or longer. Garnish with the reserved bacon pieces and chopped fresh parsley.

May be prepared up to 24 hours in advance . . . if they last that long.

Serves 4 to 6

Bacon and Egg Puff

4 cups dry bread cubes
2 cups (8 ounces) shredded Cheddar cheese
1/2 cup (2 ounces) shredded Monterey Jack cheese
10 eggs
4 cups milk
1 teaspoon salt
1 teaspoon pepper
1 teaspoon onion powder
1 teaspoon dry mustard
10 slices bacon, crisp-cooked and crumbled

Arrange the bread cubes over the bottom of a buttered 9x13-inch baking dish. Sprinkle with the Cheddar cheese and Monterey Jack cheese. Lightly whisk the eggs in a bowl and stir in the milk, salt, pepper, onion powder and dry mustard. Pour over the prepared layers and sprinkle with the bacon.

Chill, covered, for 8 to 10 hours. Bake, uncovered, in a preheated 325-degree oven for 1 hour or until set. Serve warm.

Serves 10

Ham and Asparagus Quiche

1 (9-inch) refrigerator pie pastry
1 tablespoon unsalted butter
1/3 cup chopped shallots (about 2)
8 ounces fresh asparagus
8 ounces Virginia baked ham, cut into 1-inch
    slices and chopped
1 cup (4 ounces) shredded Gruyère cheese
4 eggs
2 cups half-and-half
3/4 teaspoon salt
1/4 teaspoon freshly ground black pepper
1/8 teaspoon cayenne pepper

Fit the pastry into a 9-inch pie plate and crimp or flute the edge. Melt the butter in a large nonstick skillet over medium heat. Add the shallots and sauté for 2 minutes or until tender. Let stand until cool.

Snap off the thick woody ends of the asparagus spears and discard. Cut the spears diagonally into 1/2-inch slices. Blanch the asparagus in boiling water in a saucepan for 1 minute. Drain and let stand until cool. Scatter the shallots, asparagus and ham in the prepared pie plate. Sprinkle with the cheese.

Lightly whisk the eggs in a bowl. Add the half-and-half, salt, black pepper and cayenne pepper and stir until blended. Pour over the prepared layers. Bake in a preheated 425-degree oven for 15 minutes. Reduce the oven temperature to 300 degrees and bake for 30 minutes longer or until a knife inserted halfway into the center comes out clean. Let stand for 15 minutes before serving.

Serves 6 to 8

Southern Biscuits

2 cups self-rising flour
1 teaspoon baking powder

1/2 cup shortening
1 cup buttermilk

Mix the flour and baking powder in a bowl. Cut in the shortening using a pastry blender until crumbly. Add the buttermilk and mix well. Knead the dough four to six times on a lightly floured surface.

Roll the dough 3/4 inch thick and cut into rounds using a small biscuit cutter. Arrange the rounds on an ungreased baking sheet. Bake in a preheated 450-degree oven for 10 to 12 minutes. Broil the last minute if needed to brown.

Makes 1 dozen biscuits

Quick Pecan Rolls

2 1/2 tablespoons butter
1/3 cup packed brown sugar
1/4 cup chopped pecans
2 tablespoons water

1 (8-count) can crescent rolls
Butter, softened
2 tablespoons granulated sugar
1 to 2 teaspoons cinnamon

Melt 2 1/2 tablespoons butter in an 8-inch round baking pan in a preheated 375-degree oven. Remove from the oven. Maintain the oven temperature. Stir in the brown sugar, pecans and water until combined.

Unroll the roll dough and separate into four rectangles, pressing the perforations to seal. Spread one side of the rectangles with enough softened butter to cover. Mix the granulated sugar and cinnamon in a small bowl and sprinkle evenly over the butter. Roll the rectangles to enclose the filling, starting with the short side. Cut each roll into four slices and arrange the slices cut sides down in the prepared baking pan. Bake for 20 to 25 minutes or until golden brown.

Makes 16 small pecan rolls

Cranberry Scones with Orange-Honey Butter

Scones
3 cups all-purpose flour
1/2 cup sugar
1 tablespoon baking powder
1 1/2 teaspoons grated orange zest
1/2 teaspoon baking soda
1/2 teaspoon salt
1/4 teaspoon cinnamon
1/8 teaspoon ground allspice
3/4 cup (1 1/2 sticks) butter
1 cup buttermilk
1 cup fresh or frozen cranberries, chopped
1/2 cup coarsely chopped pecans

Orange-Honey Butter
1 cup (2 sticks) butter, softened
2 teaspoons grated orange zest
1 tablespoon honey

To prepare the scones, combine the flour, sugar, baking powder, orange zest, baking soda, salt, cinnamon and allspice in a large bowl and mix well. Cut in the butter until the mixture resembles coarse crumbs. Add the buttermilk and stir just until moistened. Fold in the cranberries and pecans.

Shape the dough into a ball on a lightly floured surface. Pat into a 3/4-inch-thick circle. Cut into rounds using a 2 1/2-inch cutter. Arrange the rounds on a baking sheet lined with baking parchment. Bake in a preheated 400-degree oven for 12 to 15 minutes or until light brown. Cool on the baking sheet for 2 minutes and remove to a wire rack.

To prepare the orange-honey butter, beat the butter, orange zest and honey in a mixing bowl until fluffy. Serve with the scones.

You may substitute dried cranberries plumped in orange juice for the fresh or frozen cranberries.

Makes 16 to 18 scones

Curried Chicken Canapés

1/2 cup flaked coconut
1/2 cup chopped almonds
8 ounces cream cheese, softened
2 tablespoons orange marmalade
1 1/2 teaspoons curry powder
1/4 teaspoon salt
1/4 teaspoon pepper
2 cups chopped cooked chicken
12 (1/2-inch-thick) slices firm pumpernickel, wheat
    or white bread
3 tablespoons finely chopped green onions

Spread the coconut and almonds on a baking sheet. Toast in a preheated 350-degree oven for 5 to 10 minutes or until light brown, stirring occasionally. Remove to a plate to cool. Mix the cream cheese, marmalade, curry powder, salt and pepper in a bowl until combined. Fold in the chicken.

Spread the chicken mixture on one side of each slice of bread. Trim the crusts and cut each bread slice into three equal strips. Sprinkle evenly with the coconut mixture and green onions. Arrange on a serving platter.

This is a lovely open-face sandwich. The quality of the bread is the key to success.

Makes 3 dozen canapés

Artichoke Cheese Spread

16 ounces cream cheese, softened
1/2 cup finely chopped green onion tops
1 cup (4 ounces) freshly grated Parmesan cheese
1 (14-ounce) can artichoke hearts, drained and
    finely chopped
2 tablespoons olive oil
1 tablespoon lemon juice
2 garlic cloves, crushed
1/2 teaspoon ground red pepper (optional)
3/4 cup jarred roasted red peppers,
    drained and chopped

Combine the cream cheese and green onions in a bowl and mix well. Mix the Parmesan cheese, artichokes, olive oil, lemon juice, garlic and red pepper in a bowl.

Line a 4-cup glass bowl with plastic wrap. Spread one-third of the cream cheese mixture in the bottom of the prepared bowl. Layer with one-half of the roasted red peppers, 3/4 cup of the artichoke mixture and one-half of the remaining cream cheese mixture. Top with the remaining roasted red peppers, remaining artichoke mixture and remaining cream cheese mixture. Chill, covered, for 2 hours or longer.

Invert onto a serving platter and discard the plastic wrap. Garnish with red and yellow bell pepper strips. Serve with assorted party crackers.

Serves 8

Classic Southern Pimento Cheese

8 ounces sharp Cheddar cheese
1 (2-ounce) jar chopped pimentos, drained
2 teaspoons finely grated red onion (optional)
3/4 teaspoon salt, or to taste
1/4 teaspoon pepper
Dash of Worcestershire sauce
1/3 cup (about) mayonnaise

Shred the cheese into a bowl; do not use preshredded cheese. Stir in the pimentos, onion, salt, pepper and Worcestershire sauce. Add the mayonnaise and stir until of a spreading consistency. Chill, covered, for 1 hour. Spread on your favorite bread.

Makes 1 1/2 cups

*P*imento cheese sandwiches are made with thin white bread, cut into halves, and crusts removed. They are served at nearly every sort of southern gathering, especially following funerals. At the beach, pimento cheese is good as a dip with corn chips.

Chicken, Basil and Cashew Pâté

10 ounces boneless skinless chicken breasts
Salt and pepper to taste
3 tablespoons butter
1 tablespoon chopped garlic
1/3 cup lightly salted roasted cashews
1/3 cup mayonnaise
1/2 cup finely chopped onion
1/4 cup (1 ounce) grated asiago cheese
1 teaspoon hot red pepper sauce, or to taste
1/4 cup chopped fresh basil

Cut the chicken into 1/2-inch pieces and sprinkle with salt and pepper. Melt the butter in a heavy skillet over medium-high heat. Add the chicken and garlic and sauté for 3 minutes or until the chicken is cooked through. Stir in the cashews. Remove from the heat and let stand until cool.

Combine the chicken mixture, mayonnaise, onion, cheese and 1 teaspoon hot sauce in a food processor and process until smooth. Add the basil and process just until blended. Season with salt, pepper and hot sauce to taste. Spoon the pâté into a small bowl and chill, covered, for 8 to 10 hours. Serve with toasted baguette slices, tomatoes and sweet gherkins. You may prepare up to 2 days in advance.

Makes 2 cups

Buttery Ham Spread

8 ounces Black Forest or Virginia baked ham
1/2 cup (1 stick) butter, softened
8 ounces cream cheese, softened
3 green onions, chopped
1 tablespoon lemon juice
1/4 teaspoon salt
1/4 teaspoon pepper

Process the ham in a food processor until finely chopped. Beat the butter and cream cheese in a mixing bowl until creamy. Fold in the ham, green onions, lemon juice, salt and pepper until combined. Taste and adjust the seasonings. Chill, covered, for 1 hour or longer.

For a smoother consistency, add the butter, cream cheese, green onions, lemon juice, salt and pepper to the ham in the food processor and pulse until combined.

Makes 2 cups

*W*onderful as a spread on sweet potato biscuits, atop chewy raisin walnut bread, or spread on crackers.

Smoked Salmon Mousse with Caviar

8 ounces smoked salmon, thinly sliced
1 1/2 cups crème fraîche or sour cream
1 tablespoon fresh lemon juice
1/4 to 1/2 teaspoon cayenne pepper, or to taste
1 (1- to 2-ounce) jar salmon caviar
Chopped chives

Process the salmon in a food processor until chopped. Add the crème fraîche, lemon juice and cayenne pepper and pulse just until mixed. Spoon into a bowl and fold in the caviar.

Chill, covered, for 2 to 10 hours. Sprinkle with chives. Serve with toast points and/or assorted party crackers.

Serves 8

No time to plan ahead? Roasted mushrooms tossed in olive oil, dried oregano, salt and pepper makes a quick low-calorie appetizer or a side dish to steak.

Cheese Krispies

2 cups all-purpose flour
1/2 teaspoon salt
1/2 teaspoon red pepper
1/2 teaspoon paprika
8 ounces sharp Cheddar cheese, shredded
3/4 cup plus 2 tablespoons butter, softened
1 1/4 cups crisp rice cereal, crushed

Sift the flour, salt, red pepper and paprika together. Mix the cheese and butter in a bowl until combined. Add the flour mixture and stir until a dough forms. Add the cereal and mix well.

Shape the dough into 1-inch balls and arrange in a single layer on an ungreased baking sheet. Flatten the balls with the bottom of a lightly floured glass. Bake in a preheated 400-degree oven for 10 minutes. Cool on the baking sheet for 2 minutes. Remove to a wire rack to cool completely. Store in an airtight container.

Makes 4 dozen krispies

Minted Fruit Salad

8 cups assorted seasonal fresh fruit,
    cut into bite-size pieces
$^1/_2$ cup tangerine juice
1 tablespoon sugar
2 tablespoons chopped fresh mint

Toss the fruit, juice and sugar in a large bowl until combined. Sprinkle with the mint. Chill, covered, until serving time. The flavor is best the day the salad is prepared.

A nice combination is melon balls, strawberries, blackberries, raspberries, chopped mangoes, and sliced kiwifruit. Feel free to use your favorite fruits or whatever is fresh, in season, and looks good.

Serves 8

Blueberry Gelatin Salad

Salad
2 (3-ounce) packages blackberry, raspberry or
    black cherry gelatin
2 cups boiling water
1 (7-ounce) can crushed pineapple
1 (21-ounce) can blueberry pie filling

Sour Cream Topping
1 cup sour cream
3 ounces cream cheese, softened
1/4 cup sugar

To prepare the salad, combine the gelatin with the boiling water in a heatproof bowl and stir until the gelatin dissolves. Let stand for 3 minutes. Stir in the undrained pineapple and pie filling. Pour the gelatin mixture into a 7x11-inch dish or a 4-cup mold. Chill until set.

To prepare the topping, beat the sour cream, cream cheese and sugar in a mixing bowl until blended. Spread over the chilled layer. Garnish with chopped nuts and fresh blueberries. Store in the refrigerator until serving time. If using a mold, invert onto a serving platter and then spread with the topping.

Serves 8

Marinated Asparagus Salad

1 pound asparagus
1/2 cup balsamic vinaigrette
1/4 cup sesame oil
1/2 cup chopped roasted red peppers

Snap off the thick woody ends of the asparagus and discard. Place the asparagus spears in a large sealable plastic bag. Add the vinaigrette and sesame oil to the bag and seal tightly. Shake to coat.

Marinate in the refrigerator for 8 to 10 hours or until the asparagus is tender-crisp, turning occasionally. Arrange the asparagus on a serving platter and sprinkle with the roasted peppers. Garnish with sesame seeds.

Serves 4 to 6

What to do with that bumper crop of cherry tomatoes? Cut them into halves and toss with some olive oil and fresh herbs. Season with a little salt and pepper, and you have a quick five-minute salad. Great with grilled steaks.

New Potato and Chive Salad

30 small new potatoes, about 1 inch in diameter
3 tablespoons olive oil
1 tablespoon white wine vinegar
1 teaspoon Dijon mustard
4 green onions, finely chopped
1/2 cup mayonnaise
3 tablespoons chopped fresh chives
Salt and pepper to taste

If any of the potatoes are larger than 1 inch, cut into halves or quarters. Cook the potatoes in boiling water in a saucepan until tender; drain. Whisk the olive oil, vinegar and Dijon mustard in a bowl until blended. Stir in the green onions. Add the hot potatoes to the olive oil mixture and toss to coat. Let stand until cool.

Add the mayonnaise and chives to the potato mixture and mix well. Season with salt and pepper. Chill, covered, until serving time.

Serves 4

This recipe originates in South Africa and is usually served with grilled chicken or chilled meats.

Warm Pancetta, Goat Cheese and Spinach Salad

6 cups loosely-packed stemmed baby spinach
5 ounces fresh goat cheese, crumbled
1/3 cup thickly sliced pancetta,
    cut into 1/4x1-inch strips
Extra-virgin olive oil
1 tablespoon minced garlic
2 teaspoons minced fresh thyme leaves
1/4 cup sherry vinegar
Sea salt and freshly ground pepper to taste

Place the spinach in a large heatproof salad bowl and sprinkle with the cheese. Cook the pancetta in a medium skillet over medium heat for 8 to 10 minutes or until crisp, stirring occasionally. Drain the pancetta through a sieve into a heatproof measuring cup, reserving the pan drippings. If the pan drippings do not measure 1/4 cup, add enough olive oil to measure 1/4 cup.

Return the pan drippings to the skillet and add the pancetta. Cook until the pancetta is heated through and then add the garlic. Cook for 30 seconds or until the garlic is light brown, stirring occasionally. Stir in the thyme and let it crackle for about 10 seconds. Mix in the vinegar, salt and pepper.

Cook for 30 seconds to lower the acidity of the vinegar; you should see tiny drops of vinegar dispersed throughout the pan drippings. Pour the hot dressing over the spinach and toss until the leaves are coated and the cheese melts slightly. Serve immediately.

Serves 6

Asian Chicken Salad with Peanut Dressing

Peanut Dressing
1/4 cup rice wine vinegar
1/4 cup canola oil
2 teaspoons chopped fresh ginger
2 tablespoons creamy peanut butter
1 tablespoon honey
1 tablespoon soy sauce
1 tablespoon toasted sesame oil
Dash of hot red pepper sauce
Salt and pepper to taste

Salad
1 (10-ounce) package angel hair
    coleslaw
1 (10-ounce) package romaine, torn
    into bite-size pieces

4 ounces blanched snow peas,
    diagonally sliced into bite-size pieces
6 baby carrots, chopped or shredded
1/2 cup sliced green onions
2 cups shredded cooked chicken
Juice of 1/2 lime

Toppings
1/2 cup roasted peanuts, coarsely
    chopped
1/4 cup chopped fresh mint
1/4 cup chopped fresh cilantro
Chopped green onions

To prepare the dressing, process the vinegar, canola oil, ginger, peanut butter, honey, soy sauce, sesame oil, hot sauce, salt and pepper in a food processor or blender until smooth. Chill, covered, in the refrigerator.

To prepare the salad, toss the coleslaw, romaine, snow peas, carrots and green onions in a large salad bowl. Top with the chicken and drizzle with the lime juice. Chill, covered, in the refrigerator before serving.

Serve the salad with the dressing and assorted toppings on the side, or add the dressing and toppings to the salad but do not toss before serving. Garnish with lime quarters.

The dressing, chicken and salad may be prepared in advance and stored, covered, in the refrigerator. The salad should not be assembled until just prior to serving, otherwise the peanuts will become soggy.

Serves 4 to 6

Blue Cheese Bow Tie Pasta Salad

4 ounces cooked ham, julienned
1 cup pecan pieces
3/4 cup crumbled blue cheese
1/3 cup snipped parsley
1/3 cup olive oil
1 garlic clove, finely minced
2 tablespoons chopped fresh rosemary, or
    2 teaspoons dried rosemary, lightly crushed
1/2 teaspoon pepper
Grated Parmesan cheese to taste
8 ounces bow tie pasta

Combine the ham, pecans, blue cheese, parsley, olive oil, garlic, rosemary, pepper and Parmesan cheese in a bowl and mix well. Let stand, covered, at room temperature for 30 minutes.

Cook the pasta using the package directions. Drain and toss the hot pasta with the ham mixture. Sprinkle with Parmesan cheese and serve immediately.

The ham mixture may be prepared in advance and stored, covered, in the refrigerator. Bring to room temperature and mix with the hot pasta just before serving.

Serves 4 to 6

*E*asy! A great addition to a luncheon salad sampler.

Bourbon-Marinated Beef Tenderloin

1 (5- to 8-pound) beef tenderloin, trimmed
Lemon pepper to taste
2 cups reduced-sodium soy sauce
1/2 cup bourbon
2 garlic cloves, crushed
3 slices bacon
1 onion, sliced

Sprinkle the tenderloin with lemon pepper and place in a large sealable plastic bag. Whisk the soy sauce, bourbon and garlic in a bowl and pour over the tenderloin. Seal tightly and turn to coat. Marinate the tenderloin in the refrigerator for 2 to 10 hours, turning occasionally. Bring to room temperature and drain, reserving the marinade.

Place the tenderloin on a rack in a shallow roasting pan. Lay the bacon on top of the tenderloin and arrange the onion over the bacon. Place the roasting pan in a preheated 450-degree oven. Reduce the oven temperature to 400 degrees and roast for 40 to 45 minutes for medium-rare or to the desired degree of doneness.

Bring the reserved marinade to a boil in a saucepan while the tenderloin is roasting. Reduce the heat and simmer until reduced by one-half or more, stirring occasionally. Discard the bacon and onion and allow the tenderloin to stand for 15 minutes before slicing. Serve with the reduced marinade on the side.

Serves 10

Beef and Scallion Bundles

4 scallions, trimmed
1 tablespoon canola oil
1 red bell pepper, cut into thin strips
1 tablespoon soy sauce
1 pound beef sirloin, cut into 8 slices
Coarse salt and freshly ground pepper to taste
1 tablespoon canola oil
2 tablespoons water
2 tablespoons soy sauce
1 tablespoon rice vinegar
2 teaspoons sugar
Hot cooked rice

Thinly slice the scallions lengthwise and then cut into 2-inch pieces. Heat 1 tablespoon canola oil in a large nonstick skillet over medium-high heat. Add the bell pepper and cook for 2 to 4 minutes or until the bell pepper blisters, shaking the skillet frequently. Stir in 1 tablespoon soy sauce. Remove to a plate and wipe the skillet clean.

Pound the beef slices 1/8 inch thick between sheets of plastic wrap. Season with salt and pepper. Sprinkle the scallions and bell pepper evenly over the slices and roll each slice into a bundle. Secure with wooden picks.

Heat 1 tablespoon canola oil in the same skillet over high heat. Sear the bundles in two batches in the hot oil for 3 to 4 minutes or until brown on all sides. Remove the bundles to a platter and cover to keep warm. Wipe the skillet clean. Combine the water, 2 tablespoons soy sauce, the vinegar and sugar in the skillet.

Cook over medium heat for 2 to 3 minutes or until the mixture is reduced to a syrupy consistency, stirring constantly. Remove the wooden picks from the bundles and drizzle with the sauce. Serve over rice.

Serves 4

This would make a great appetizer. Just omit the rice and cut the bundles into one-inch pinwheels.

Pineapple-Glazed Ham

1 (4-pound) cured ham
1 (8-ounce) can juice-pack crushed pineapple
1/2 cup packed brown sugar
2 tablespoons honey
1 tablespoon dry mustard
2 tablespoons cornstarch

Arrange the ham fat side up on a sheet of foil large enough to enclose the ham and place in a shallow roasting pan. Wrap the foil loosely around the ham. Bake in a preheated 325-degree oven for 1 hour and 10 minutes. Remove the ham from the oven and maintain the oven temperature

Combine the pineapple, brown sugar, honey, dry mustard and cornstarch in a saucepan and mix well. Bring to a boil over medium heat and boil for 1 minute, stirring constantly. Spoon the pineapple glaze over the ham and return the ham to the oven. Increase the oven temperature to 375 degrees and bake, uncovered, for 30 minutes or until the glaze is bubbly, basting frequently with the pan drippings.

Serves 8

Chicken and Asparagus Casserole

2 pounds fresh asparagus
Salt to taste
2 (2- to 2^1/2-pound) rotisserie chickens
^{1}/2 cup (1 stick) unsalted butter
^{1}/2 cup all-purpose flour
3 cups chicken stock
1 cup half-and-half
12 ounces mushrooms, chopped
^{1}/2 cup dry white wine
1 teaspoon salt
1 teaspoon white pepper
1^1/2 cups (6 ounces) freshly grated
    Parmesan cheese
1 cup slivered almonds, toasted
Hot cooked rice

Snap off the woody ends of the asparagus and discard. Cut the spears into 1-inch pieces. Cook the asparagus in boiling salted water in a saucepan for exactly 6 minutes. Drain and rinse with cold water to stop the cooking process and preserve the green color. Chop the chicken into bite-size pieces, discarding the skin and bones.

Melt the butter in a saucepan over medium heat. Stir in the flour and cook for 5 minutes or until bubbly, stirring constantly. Whisk in the stock and bring to a boil. Reduce the heat to medium-low. Stir in the half-and-half and simmer for 10 minutes or until smooth and thickened. Add the chicken, mushrooms, wine, 1 teaspoon salt and the pepper. Taste and adjust the seasonings. Add the asparagus and mix gently.

Spoon into a 9×13-inch baking dish. Sprinkle with the cheese and almonds. Bake in a preheated 325-degree oven for 30 minutes. Serve over rice or spoon into puff pastry shells for a nice presentation.

Serves 8

Cache Chicken

4 boneless skinless chicken breasts, chilled
4 (^{1}/4×1^1/2×3-inch) slices Monterey Jack cheese
2 eggs
3/4 cup all-purpose flour
1 tablespoon minced fresh parsley, or
    1 teaspoon parsley flakes
^{1}/2 teaspoon salt
^{1}/2 teaspoon paprika
^{1}/2 teaspoon garlic salt
^{1}/4 teaspoon pepper
^{1}/4 teaspoon dried sage (optional)
^{1}/2 cup (2 ounces) finely grated fresh
    Parmesan cheese
^{1}/4 cup (^{1}/2 stick) butter

Cut a pocket lengthwise in the side of each chicken breast with a sharp knife. Place one slice of Monterey Jack cheese inside each pocket and secure with wooden picks. Chill for 15 to 30 minutes or until cold.

Whisk the eggs in a shallow dish until blended. Combine the flour, parsley, salt, paprika, garlic salt, pepper and sage in a sealable plastic bag and seal tightly. Shake to mix. Carefully place the chicken in the bag and seal tightly. Shake gently until the chicken is coated with the flour mixture. Dip the chicken in the egg and sprinkle with the Parmesan cheese. Chill for 15 to 30 minutes.

Melt the butter in a skillet over medium heat and add the chicken. Sauté for 10 to 12 minutes on each side or until golden brown and cooked through. Remove to a serving platter and garnish with lemon slices and/or sprigs of parsley. Serve immediately.

Serves 4

Chicken with Sun-Dried Tomato Sauce

2 ounces dried sun-dried tomatoes
1 tablespoon butter
1 garlic clove, minced
3/4 cup chicken stock
1 cup heavy cream
4 boneless skinless chicken breasts
Salt and freshly ground pepper to taste
2 tablespoons olive oil
1/4 cup chicken stock
2 tablespoons chopped fresh basil
Hot cooked rice or fettuccini

Chop the tomatoes into bite-size pieces. Melt the butter in a saucepan over low heat and add the garlic. Cook for 1 minute. Stir in the tomatoes and 3/4 cup stock and bring to a boil over high heat. Reduce the heat to medium and simmer for 10 minutes or until the tomatoes are tender, stirring occasionally. Add the cream and bring to a boil, stirring constantly. Reduce the heat and simmer until the sauce is thick enough to coat the back of a spoon.

Sprinkle the surface of the chicken with salt and pepper. Heat the olive oil in a skillet over medium-high heat and add the chicken. Sauté for 4 to 5 minutes on each side or until cooked through. Remove the chicken to a platter using a slotted spoon and cover to keep warm.

Discard any fat from the skillet and add 1/4 cup stock. Bring to a boil, stirring with a wooden spoon to dislodge any browned bits on the bottom of the skillet. Cook until slightly reduced and then stir into the tomato sauce. Stir in the basil and adjust the seasonings. Slice the chicken on the diagonal and arrange over hot cooked rice or fettuccini on serving plates. Drizzle with the tomato sauce and serve.

Serves 4

Salmon with Tomatoes, Basil and White Beans

1 onion, coarsely chopped
1 tablespoon olive oil
1 (15-ounce) can cannellini beans, drained and rinsed
1 cup grape tomato halves
1/2 cup chopped pitted kalamata olives (optional)
2 tablespoon chopped fresh basil
4 (6-ounce) salmon fillets
1/2 teaspoon salt
1/2 teaspoon pepper
1 tablespoon olive oil

Sauté the onion in 1 tablespoon olive oil in a saucepan over medium heat for 2 minutes or until slightly softened. Stir in the beans, tomatoes and olives. Cook over medium heat for 2 minutes or until heated through, stirring occasionally. Remove from the heat and stir in the basil. Cover to keep warm.

Sprinkle the salmon evenly with the salt and pepper. Heat 1 tablespoon olive oil in a large nonstick skillet over medium-high heat. Cook the salmon in the hot oil for 3 minutes per side or until the salmon flakes easily. Arrange one salmon fillet on each of four serving plates and top each fillet with one-fourth of the bean mixture. Serve immediately.

Serves 4

Barbecued Salmon with Cucumber Salsa

Cucumber Salsa
1 English cucumber, chopped
1 green onion, thinly sliced
1 tablespoon chopped fresh mint
1/4 cup seasoned rice wine vinegar
2 cups strawberries, chopped

Barbecue Sauce and Salmon
1/2 cup (1 stick) unsalted butter
1 garlic clove, minced
2 tablespoons honey
2 tablespoons soy sauce
1 tablespoon fresh lemon juice
Salmon fillets

To prepare the salsa, combine the cucumber, green onion, mint and vinegar in a bowl and mix well. Stir in the strawberries. Chill, covered, in the refrigerator.

To prepare the sauce, melt the butter in a small saucepan. Add the garlic and cook over low heat, stirring constantly. Stir in the honey, soy sauce and lemon juice and bring to a low boil, stirring constantly. Baste salmon fillets with the sauce and grill or broil until the fillets flake easily, basting with the remaining sauce occasionally. Serve with the salsa.

Variable servings

This is a wonderful springtime recipe when strawberries are in season. Lemony Rice on page 221 makes a delicious accompaniment.

Crab Cakes

Béchamel Sauce
1 tablespoon butter
1 tablespoon all-purpose flour
1/2 cup milk
Salt to taste

Crab Cakes
1 pound lump or back-fin crab meat,
    shells removed and crab meat flaked
2 tablespoons fresh lemon juice
2 eggs, beaten
2 tablespoons mayonnaise
2 teaspoons Worcestershire sauce

1/4 cup dry bread crumbs
1 teaspoon salt
1 teaspoon dry mustard
1/8 teaspoon white pepper

Breading and Assembly
1 cup dry bread crumbs
1 teaspoon paprika
1/4 cup milk
1 egg
1/2 cup all-purpose flour
1/2 to 1 cup vegetable oil

To prepare the sauce, melt the butter in a small saucepan over low heat. Stir in the flour and cook for 1 minute, stirring constantly. Add the milk gradually and cook until thickened and smooth, stirring or whisking constantly. Remove from the heat and season with salt.

To prepare the crab cakes, gently toss the crab meat with the lemon juice in a bowl. Whisk the eggs in a bowl until blended. Add the béchamel sauce gradually to avoid curdling the eggs and mix until blended. Stir in the mayonnaise, Worcestershire sauce, bread crumbs, salt, dry mustard and white pepper. Fold in the crab meat. Chill until firm. Shape the crab meat mixture into ten to twelve 3-inch cakes.

To prepare the breading, mix the bread crumbs and paprika in a shallow dish. Whisk the milk and egg in a shallow dish until blended. Coat the crab cakes with the flour, dip in the egg wash and coat with the bread crumb mixture. Arrange on a baking sheet lined with waxed paper and chill for 30 minutes.

Heat 1/2 cup oil in a large nonstick skillet over medium heat for 3 to 4 minutes. Sauté the crab cakes in batches in the hot oil for 3 to 4 minutes per side or until light brown and heated through, adding the remaining oil as needed. Drain on paper towels. Serve with lemon wedges, tartar sauce and/or rémoulade sauce. The crab cakes may be reheated in a 300-degree oven for 5 minutes just before serving if needed.

Makes 10 to 12 crab cakes

*H*omemade Rémoulade Sauce on page 194 is a wonderful and easy accompaniment to this recipe.

Baked Lemon Shrimp

1/2 cup (1 stick) unsalted butter
1/3 cup Worcestershire sauce
2 sprigs of fresh rosemary
2 teaspoons garlic juice
1 teaspoon thyme
1 teaspoon pepper
1/2 teaspoon celery salt
1 pound deveined peeled shrimp
1 small lemon, thinly sliced and seeded
1/2 cup unseasoned bread crumbs
1/3 cup grated Parmesan cheese

Combine the butter, Worcestershire sauce, rosemary, garlic juice, thyme, pepper and celery salt in a small saucepan. Cook over low heat for 5 minutes, stirring occasionally. Discard the rosemary sprigs.

Arrange the shrimp in a single layer in a shallow baking dish. Pour the butter mixture over the shrimp. Top with the lemon slices and sprinkle with the bread crumbs and cheese. Bake in a preheated 400-degree oven for 15 minutes or until the shrimp turn pink.

Wonderful served over Cheese Grits on page 120.

Serves 4

Pasta Primavera

12 ounces fresh spaghetti, linguini or
    angel hair pasta
5 tablespoons extra-virgin olive oil
3 or 4 large garlic cloves, minced
1 tablespoon parsley flakes
1 (16-ounce) can petite diced tomatoes
1 small yellow squash, thinly sliced
1 small zucchini, thinly sliced
3/4 cup broccoli florets, chopped
3/4 cup cauliflower florets, chopped
3/4 cup white mushrooms, sliced
Salt and pepper to taste
Freshly grated Parmesan cheese to taste

Cook the pasta using the package directions. Drain and cover to keep warm. Heat the olive oil in a 2-quart saucepan over medium heat. Add the garlic and sauté until golden brown. Stir in the parsley flakes and sauté for 1 minute. Add the tomatoes and mix well.

Simmer over low heat for 25 minutes, stirring occasionally. Stir in the yellow squash, zucchini, broccoli, cauliflower and mushrooms. Simmer, covered, for 6 to 8 minutes or until the vegetables are tender. Season with salt and pepper. Spoon over the hot cooked pasta on a platter. Sprinkle with cheese and serve immediately.

Makes 3 generous servings

Roasted Green Beans

1 tablespoon olive oil
1 pound fresh green beans, trimmed
1 cup thinly sliced red onion
10 garlic cloves
2 tablespoons olive oil
Salt and pepper to taste
1/2 cup pine nuts, lightly toasted
1 to 2 teaspoons balsamic vinegar (optional)

Line a baking sheet with sides with foil and brush the foil with 1 tablespoon olive oil. Spread the beans, onion and garlic on the prepared baking sheet. Brush the beans, onion and garlic with 2 tablespoons olive oil using a basting brush. Sprinkle with salt and pepper.

Roast in a preheated 400-degree oven for 20 minutes, stirring every 5 minutes. Mix in the pine nuts and roast for 5 minutes longer. Spoon into a bowl and drizzle with the vinegar. Sprinkle with pepper.

Serves 4 to 6

Green beans are easy to prepare in advance. Blanch the beans in boiling water and then plunge into an ice water bath to stop the cooking process and preserve the green color. Reheat the beans in melted butter just before serving. Add toasted almonds to make an elegant side dish for your holiday table.

Onion Tart

1 (9-inch) refrigerator pie pastry
1 tablespoon virgin olive oil
1 1/2 sweet yellow onions, thinly sliced
1/2 cup plus 2 tablespoons heavy cream
1/2 cup plus 2 tablespoons milk
2 eggs
Salt and pepper to taste
Pinch of grated nutmeg
4 ounces Gruyère cheese, shredded

Fit the pie pastry in an 8-inch pie plate and flute or crimp the edge. Bake in a preheated 350-degree oven for 5 minutes. Deflate any air bubbles with a sharp knife and continue baking for 10 minutes longer or just until the shell begins to crisp. Let stand until cool. Increase the oven temperature to 375 degrees.

Heat the olive oil in a skillet and add the onions. Sauté for 5 minutes or until the onions are tender. Remove to a plate to cool. Whisk the cream, milk, eggs, salt, pepper and nutmeg in a bowl until frothy. Spread the onions in the baked pie shell and sprinkle with the cheese. Pour the cream mixture over the top. Bake for 30 minutes. Let cool to lukewarm before serving.

Serves 4 to 6

Serve as a light first course or as a side dish to grilled steaks.

Sweet Potato Soufflé

Soufflé
6 to 8 sweet potatoes
1 cup sugar
1 cup milk
2/3 cup butter, melted
3 eggs, lightly beaten
2 teaspoons vanilla extract

Topping
1 1/2 cups shredded coconut
1 1/2 cups chopped pecans
1 1/2 cups packed brown sugar
2/3 cup all-purpose flour
2/3 cup butter, melted

To prepare the soufflé, arrange the sweet potatoes on a baking sheet. Bake in a preheated 400-degree oven for about 45 minutes or until tender. Maintain the oven temperature. Peel the sweet potatoes and mash the pulp in a bowl. Combine 6 cups of the mashed sweet potatoes with the sugar, milk, butter, eggs and vanilla in a bowl and mix well. Reserve any unused mashed sweet potatoes for another use. Spread the sweet potato mixture in a greased 9×13-inch baking dish.

To prepare the topping, toss the coconut, pecans, brown sugar, flour and butter in a bowl until combined. Sprinkle over the prepared layer and bake for 20 minutes.

A favorite menu item served at Faculty and Staff Appreciation Luncheons.

Serves 8 to 10

*S*weet potatoes are a great nutrient-packed food. Make them lower in calories and part of your weekday repertoire by cutting them into chunks, tossing with a little olive oil, salt and pepper, and roasting until they are crusty on the outside and soft on the inside.

Couscous à la Grecque

1 tablespoon olive oil
2 Japanese eggplant, trimmed and cut into
    1/2-inch pieces
1 (9-ounce) package frozen artichoke
    hearts, thawed
1 red onion, chopped
1 zucchini, cut into 1/2-inch pieces
1 red bell pepper, cut into 1/2-inch pieces
4 large garlic cloves, chopped
1 1/4 cups canned no-salt-added chicken broth
1 1/4 teaspoons dried oregano, crushed
1/2 teaspoon dried thyme
1 cup couscous
Salt and pepper to taste
3 ounces feta cheese, coarsely crumbled
1 cup chopped seeded plum tomatoes
1/3 cup chopped fresh mint

Heat the olive oil in a large saucepan or Dutch oven over high heat. Stir in the eggplant, artichokes, onion, zucchini, bell pepper and garlic. Sauté for 10 to 12 minutes or just until the vegetables are tender. Add the broth, oregano and thyme and bring to a boil. Stir in the couscous. Turn off the heat. Let stand, covered, for 10 minutes.

Season the couscous with salt and pepper. Add the cheese, tomatoes and mint and mix well. Serve warm with pita bread.

Serves 4 to 6

Apricot Rice Pilaf

2 cups chicken broth
1 cup long grain rice
3 tablespoons butter
1 small onion, chopped
1/2 cup chopped celery
1 (1/2-inch) piece fresh ginger, minced
1/4 cup chopped dried apricots
2 tablespoons apricot preserves
1 (1/4-inch) piece fresh ginger, minced
2 teaspoons cider vinegar
Salt and freshly ground pepper to taste
1/2 cup slivered almonds
2 tablespoons minced fresh parsley

Mix the broth and rice in a saucepan and let stand for 30 minutes. Melt the butter in a small saucepan and add the onion, celery and minced 1/2-inch piece ginger. Sauté over medium heat for 5 minutes or until the vegetables are soft but not brown. Add the onion mixture, apricots, preserves, minced 1/4-inch piece ginger and the vinegar to the rice mixture and mix well.

Bring to a boil and then reduce the heat. Simmer, covered, for 25 minutes or until the rice is tender. Season with salt and pepper. Spoon the rice into a serving bowl and sprinkle with the almonds and parsley. Serve immediately.

Serves 6

Kentucky Butter Cake

Cake
3 cups all-purpose flour
1 teaspoon baking powder
1 teaspoon salt
$1/2$ teaspoon baking soda
1 cup buttermilk
2 teaspoons vanilla extract
2 cups sugar
1 cup (2 sticks) butter
4 eggs

Butter Sauce
1 cup sugar
$1/2$ cup (1 stick) butter
$1/4$ cup water
$1/2$ teaspoon vanilla extract

To prepare the cake, sift the flour, baking powder, salt and baking soda together. Mix the buttermilk and vanilla together in a measuring cup. Beat the sugar and butter in a mixing bowl until creamy. Add the eggs one at a time, beating well after each addition. Add the buttermilk mixture alternately with the dry ingredients, mixing well after each addition.

Spoon the batter into a greased tube pan. Bake in a preheated 325-degree oven for 60 to 65 minutes or until the cake tests done. Pierce the top of the hot cake with a wooden skewer.

To prepare the sauce, combine the sugar, butter, water and vanilla in a small saucepan. Cook until blended, stirring occasionally; do not allow to boil. Pour the hot sauce over the hot cake. Let stand in the pan until cool. Remove to a cake plate. Although this cake is wonderful just after being baked, the flavor is even better the following day.

Serves 12

Chocolate Strawberry Decadence

10 (1 1/2-ounce) good-quality dark chocolate
    candy bars, finely chopped
5 eggs
1 cup sugar
1/2 cup (1 stick) unsalted butter, melted
Pinch of salt
Confectioners' sugar for dusting
Sliced fresh strawberries
Whipped cream

Microwave the chocolate in a microwave-safe bowl for 45 seconds. Let stand for 30 seconds and gently whisk until blended. Continue to microwave in 10-second intervals until the chocolate is melted if needed

Beat the eggs in a mixing bowl at medium speed until blended. Gradually add the sugar, beating constantly at medium-high speed for 2 minutes or until light and fluffy. Beat in the butter and salt. Add the chocolate and mix until blended.

Fill twelve generously buttered miniature bundt cups or twelve generously buttered muffin cups three-fourths full. If there is leftover batter, a second pan may be required. Place the pan on the center oven rack in a preheated 375-degree oven. Bake for 18 to 22 minutes or until the cakes are puffed and a wooden pick inserted in the center of the cakes comes out with a few moist crumbs attached. Do not overbake.

Cool in the pans for 30 minutes; the cakes will fall slightly. Remove to a wire rack and dust with confectioners' sugar. Top with strawberries and whipped cream and serve.

Makes 1 dozen cakes

These are rich, sinful, flourless miniature chocolate cakes. Freeze for future use, if desired.

French Cream Cake

Cake
1 cup sugar
3 eggs, beaten
2 tablespoons cold water
1 1/2 cups all-purpose flour, sifted
1 teaspoon baking powder
1/4 teaspoon salt

Custard Filling
1 cup plus 2 tablespoons milk
3/4 cup sugar
2 tablespoons cornstarch
1/2 cup cold milk
2 eggs, beaten
1/2 cup (1 stick) butter, cut into
    small pieces
1 teaspoon vanilla extract

Chocolate Topping
1 ounce unsweetened chocolate
2 tablespoons margarine, melted
1 cup confectioners' sugar
1 tablespoon milk

To prepare the cake, beat the sugar, eggs and cold water in a mixing bowl until blended. Add the flour and mix well. Stir in the baking powder and salt. Do not overmix. Spread the batter evenly in two 9-inch cake pans lined with waxed paper. Bake in a preheated 375-degree oven for 12 to 15 minutes or until the cakes test done. Remove to a sheet of waxed paper and let stand until cool. Cut the layers horizontally into halves using a long, thin serrated knife.

To prepare the filling, heat 1 cup plus 2 tablespoons milk in a heavy saucepan over medium heat. Whisk in a mixture of the sugar and cornstarch. Add 1/2 cup cold milk and the eggs and mix well. Cook for 25 minutes or until thickened and the consistency of pudding, stirring occasionally. Remove from the heat and whisk to disperse any lumps. Add the butter and stir until incorporated. Let cool slightly and then stir in the vanilla. Let stand until lukewarm before proceeding.

Place the top of one cake layer cut side up on a cake plate. Spread with one-third of the custard. Layer with the bottom of the layer and spread with one-half of the remaining custard. Top with the bottom half of the remaining layer and spread with the remaining custard. End with the remaining cake layer cut side down.

To prepare the topping, heat the chocolate and margarine in a saucepan over low heat until blended, stirring occasionally. Add the confectioners' sugar and milk and stir until of a spreading consistency. Spread over the top of the cake. Chill for 8 to 10 hours.

Serves 12

White Chocolate
Lemon Curd Layer Cake

Lemon Curd

12 egg yolks, beaten
2 cups sugar
1 cup fresh lemon juice
1 cup (2 sticks) butter, chilled and
    cut into small pieces
1/4 cup grated lemon zest

1/2 cup (1 stick) butter
4 egg yolks, at room temperature
1/2 cup heavy cream
2/3 cup milk
1 teaspoon vanilla extract
4 egg whites, at room temperature
1 cup sugar

Cake

2 3/4 cups cake flour
1 teaspoon baking powder
3/4 teaspoon salt
4 ounces high-quality white chocolate
1/2 cup heavy cream
1 cup sugar

White Chocolate Cream Cheese
Frosting

9 ounces high-quality white chocolate
12 ounces cream cheese, softened
3/4 cup (1 1/2 sticks) unsalted
    butter, softened
1 1/2 teaspoons fresh lemon juice

To prepare the lemon curd, combine the egg yolks, sugar and lemon juice in a heavy nonreactive saucepan. Cook over very low heat for 20 to 25 minutes or until the consistency of pudding, stirring constantly with a wooden spoon. Remove from the heat and immediately whisk in the butter and lemon zest until incorporated. Cool over an ice bath. Store, covered, in the refrigerator for up to 3 days. This recipe only requires 2 cups of the curd.

To prepare the cake, sift the cake flour, baking powder and salt together. Combine the white chocolate and 1/2 cup cream in a double boiler. Cook over simmering water until blended, stirring occasionally. Let stand until cool. Cream 1 cup sugar and the butter in a mixing bowl until light and fluffy. Add the egg yolks one at a time, beating well after each addition. Stir 1/2 cup cream, the milk and vanilla into the white chocolate mixture. Alternately add the dry ingredients and white chocolate mixture to the creamed mixture, beating well after each addition.

Beat the egg whites in a mixing bowl until soft peaks form. Add 1 cup sugar gradually, beating constantly until stiff peaks form. Fold the egg whites into the batter. Spread the batter evenly in three greased and floured 9-inch cake pans. Bake in a preheated 350-degree oven for 25 to 30 minutes or until a skewer inserted in the middle of the layers comes out clean. Cool in the pans for 10 minutes. Remove to a wire rack to cool completely.

Spring Break

To prepare the frosting, melt the white chocolate in a double boiler over simmering water. Beat the cream cheese and white chocolate in a mixing bowl until smooth. Add the butter and lemon juice and beat until light and smooth and of a spreading consistency.

Place one of the cake layers on a cake plate and spread with a thin layer of the frosting and 1 cup of the curd. Top with another cake layer, a thin layer of the frosting and 1 cup of the curd. Top with the remaining cake layer. Spread a thin layer of the frosting over the top and side of the cake. Chill until slightly hardened. Generously spread the top and side of the cake with the remaining frosting. This will prevent any crumbs or lemon curd from showing through the frosting. Garnish with lemon slices, mint leaves and a swirl of lemon curd. Store in the refrigerator.

Serves 12 to 16

Mexican Brownies

Brownies
4 ounces unsweetened
  chocolate, chopped
1/2 cup (1 stick) unsalted butter
1 1/4 cups packed light brown sugar
1 tablespoon cinnamon
1/4 teaspoon salt
3 eggs
1 teaspoon vanilla extract

3/4 cup all-purpose flour
1 cup (6 ounces) milk chocolate chips

Brown Sugar Topping
1 cup packed brown sugar
1/4 cup whipping cream
1 tablespoon unsalted butter
3/4 teaspoon vanilla extract
1/2 cup sliced almonds

To prepare the brownies, heat the chocolate and butter in a heavy saucepan over low heat until blended, stirring occasionally. Cool for 5 minutes. Whisk in the brown sugar, cinnamon and salt. Add the eggs one at a time, whisking until blended after each addition. Stir in the vanilla. Whisk in the flour just until blended. Stir in the chocolate chips. Spread the batter in a foil-lined 8×8-inch baking pan. Bake in a preheated 325-degree oven for 35 minutes.

To prepare the topping, combine the brown sugar, cream and butter in a small heavy saucepan. Bring to a boil over low heat, whisking constantly until smooth. Remove from the heat and stir in the vanilla. Cool for 10 minutes. Whisk until of a spreading consistency. Spread the topping over the brownies and sprinkle with the almonds. Let stand for 1 hour or until set. Cut into squares and serve with cinnamon ice cream. Store the brownies in an airtight container.

Makes 16 brownies

Mint Meringue Cookies

2 egg whites
2/3 cup sugar
1/4 teaspoon cream of tartar
1/2 teaspoon peppermint extract
Green food coloring
1 cup (6 ounces) miniature mint chocolate chips or
    miniature chocolate chips

Beat the egg whites, sugar and cream of tartar in a mixing bowl until stiff peaks form, adding the flavoring and food coloring during the beating process. Fold in the chocolate chips.

Drop by spoonfuls onto a greased cookie sheet or onto a cookie sheet lined with greased baking parchment. Place the cookies in a preheated 350-degree oven. Immediately turn off the oven. Let stand with the door closed for 2 to 10 hours. Store in an airtight container.

Makes 3 dozen cookies

*C*ocktails as a dessert? Why not? Try blending coffee ice cream with equal parts of rum and Kahlúa. Cool and refreshing.

Oatmeal Lace Cookies

1/2 cup (1 stick) butter, melted
1 cup sugar
1 cup old-fashioned oats
1 egg, lightly beaten
1/2 teaspoon vanilla extract
2 tablespoons all-purpose flour
1/4 teaspoon baking powder
1/4 teaspoon salt

Combine the butter, sugar and oats in a bowl and mix well. Mix in the egg and vanilla. Stir in a mixture of the flour, baking powder and salt.

Drop by scant teaspoonfuls 4 inches apart onto a foil-lined cookie sheet. Bake in a preheated 350-degree oven for 7 to 10 minutes or until light brown. Let stand until cool. Carefully remove the cookies from the foil; roll off the edge of the counter if needed

Makes 30 cookies

To make fancy holiday cookies, remove the cookies from the oven and let stand for just thirty seconds. Shape the warm cookies around a wooden dowel to resemble a cigar. Dip the edges in melted sweet baking chocolate and let cool.

Angus Barn Key Lime Cheesecake

Graham Cracker Crust

Butter for coating
1 3/4 cups graham cracker crumbs
1/4 cup sugar
1/2 teaspoon salt
1/2 cup (1 stick) unsalted butter, melted

Lime Custard

6 egg yolks, beaten
3/4 cup sugar
6 tablespoons fresh Key lime juice
1 teaspoon grated Key lime zest

Lime Filling

16 ounces cream cheese, softened
2/3 cup plus 3 tablespoons sugar
2 eggs
3 tablespoons fresh Key lime juice
1 tablespoon grated Key lime zest

Creamy Topping

2 cups heavy whipping cream
6 ounces sweetened condensed milk
1/2 cup Key lime juice
1 (3-ounce) package vanilla instant pudding mix

To prepare the crust, wrap three layers of foil tightly over the outside bottom and side of an 8- or 8 1/2-inch springform pan with a 3-inch side. Coat the inside bottom and side with butter. Combine the graham cracker crumbs, sugar and salt in a bowl and mix well. Add the melted butter and stir until moistened. Pat over the bottom and 1 1/2 inches up the side of the prepared pan. Bake in a preheated 350-degree oven for 5 minutes or just until set. Let stand until cool. Maintain the oven temperature.

To prepare the custard, combine the egg yolks, sugar, lime juice and lime zest in a heavy saucepan. Cook over medium heat until the custard thickens and boils for 30 seconds, whisking constantly. Cool to room temperature, stirring occasionally; the custard will continue to thicken. Spread over the baked layer to within 1/4 inch of the edge.

To prepare the filling, beat the cream cheese, sugar, eggs, lime juice and lime zest in a mixing bowl until creamy. Spread over the prepared layers. Set the springform pan in a large baking pan and add enough hot water to the baking pan to come 1 inch up the side of the springform pan. Bake for about 45 minutes or until the filling is almost set but not puffed and the center jiggles slightly when the pan is gently shaken. Let stand until cool. Chill, covered, for 8 to 10 hours. Remove the side of the pan and place the cheesecake on a cake plate.

To prepare the topping, beat the cream in a mixing bowl until stiff peaks form. Combine the condensed milk, lime juice and pudding mix in a bowl and mix until smooth. Fold into the whipped cream. Spread over the top of the cheesecake. Store, covered, in the refrigerator.

Serves 12

Since 1960 the Angus Barn and the Eure family have been known for their excellent food and kind generosity throughout our community. Although steaks are the standard fare for their patrons, the restaurant is also known for its signature desserts, such as Key Lime Cheesecake. This culinary creation is a legacy of Chef Betty Shugart, whose legendary career with the Angus Barn dates back to 1965.

Strawberries with Grand Marnier Sauce

1 cup milk
1 cup heavy cream
1 teaspoon vanilla extract
4 egg yolks
$^1/_2$ cup sugar
$^1/_4$ cup Grand Marnier
1 quart strawberries

Heat the milk, cream and vanilla in a double boiler over simmering water until hot but not boiling. Whisk the egg yolks and sugar in a bowl. Stir a small amount of the hot milk mixture into the egg yolks; stir the egg yolks into the hot milk mixture gradually.

Cook for 10 minutes or until the sauce coats the back of a spoon. Do not allow to boil or the sauce will curdle. Remove from the heat and then stir in the liqueur. The sauce will continue to thicken as it cools.

Cut the strawberries into halves or slices. Spoon the strawberries evenly into four wine goblets, martini glasses or dessert bowls. Drizzle the sauce over the strawberries. The sauce may be served warm or chilled.

Serves 4

Raspberry Dessert Sauce

1 (10-ounce) package frozen raspberries
   (organic if available)
1 (12-ounce) jar seedless raspberry jam
3/4 cup sugar
1/4 cup water
1 (10-ounce) package frozen raspberries
   (organic if available)

Combine one package of raspberries, the jam, sugar and water in a small saucepan. Bring to a boil over medium heat, stirring occasionally. Reduce the heat and simmer for 4 minutes, stirring occasionally.

Remove from the heat and stir in one package of raspberries. Let stand until cool. Serve as a topping for cheesecake or ice cream. Store, covered, in the refrigerator.

A favorite menu item served at Faculty and Staff Appreciation Luncheons.

Makes 2 cups

"A sweet little Violet, blooming beneath her fair sovereign, the Rose…" begins the poem "Modesty" from *A Wreath from the Woods of Carolina*, the first children's book written by a North Carolinian. The author was Mary Ann Bryan Mason, wife of the Rev. Richard S. Mason, the Rector at Christ Church when the seeds were first planted for the establishment of Ravenscroft School. How fitting that, today, the delightful fragrances and bright, colorful hues of roses greet students on campus, their blooms seeming to signal the eminent close of another school year.

Perhaps most eager for the school year to end are the seniors. On Graduation Day, commencement speakers challenge and inspire graduates, who toss their mortar boards of Ravenscroft green and gold high into the summer air only to replace them with caps emblazoned with the colors of their college choices. Throughout its rich history, the School has been fortunate to attract many renowned guest speakers to campus for this momentous occasion, including then-Vice-President Gerald R. Ford, Mr. James J. Kilpatrick, Mr. William F. Buckley, Jr., Mrs. Elizabeth H. Dole, and Mr. Charles Kuralt.

As the weeks following graduation progress into summer, the sun's warmth, coupled with warm ocean breezes or fresh mountain air, provides the perfect setting for lighter fare, seafood, fresh fruit, and vegetables from the garden. On the following pages, you will find ideal recipes to accentuate your summer fun, from Peppered Tuna Medallions and Grilled Asian Asparagus that will become blessed last-minute family favorites, to Spice-Rubbed Baby Back Ribs and Tomato Zucchini Tart that your guests will beg you to serve again and again. So, set up the game table on the porch, fire up the grill, and treat family and friends to some delicious summer fare and fun.

Graduation

Chapter Index

Baked Blueberry Pecan French Toast

Blueberry Muffin Coffee Cake

Lemon Raspberry Muffins

Raging Crescent Rolls

Caprese Skewers

Seven-Layer Mexican Dip

Mango Salsa

Marinated Shrimp

Skewered Flank Steak

Creole Chicken Cakes with
    Rémoulade Sauce

Cheesy Crab Meat Cups

Grilled Ginger Shrimp

Chicken Lettuce Wraps

Smoked Turkey Wraps

Jammin' Turkey Sandwiches

Shrimp and Avocado Gazpacho

Asian Salad with Sesame Ginger Dressing

Thai Cabbage Salad

Grilled Corn Salad

Cucumber Scallion Salad

Red, White and Blue Salad

Balsamic Potato Salad

Chinese Chicken Salad

Marinated Shrimp and Avocado Salad

Marinated Flank Steak

Balsamic-Glazed Steaks

Grilled Honey-Soy Pork Loin

Spice-Rubbed Baby Back Ribs

Lemon Herb-Grilled Chicken and
    Vegetable Kabobs

Spicy Tuna Teriyaki

Peppered Tuna Medallions

Angel Hair Pasta with Fresh Tomato Sauce

Million-Dollar Marinade

Grilled Asian Asparagus

Ultimate Baked Beans

Tomato Zucchini Tart

Lemony Rice

Buttermilk-Glazed Carrot Cake

Fresh Plum Cake

Milk Chocolate Chip Pound Cake

Lime-Glazed Pound Cake

Best-Ever Chocolate Chip Cookies

Cracked Sugar Cookies

Holden's Barbecue Banana Pudding

Peach and Blueberry Compote

Blueberry Sour Cream Cake

Easy Peach Cobbler

Menus

Graduation Celebration

Caprese Skewers

Lemon Herb-Grilled Chicken and
    Vegetable Kabobs

Lemony Rice

Lime-Glazed Pound Cake

Easy Beach House Supper

Mango Salsa

Peppered Tuna Medallions

Asian Salad with Sesame Ginger Dressing

Peach and Blueberry Compote over
    Vanilla Ice Cream

2006 Tobacco Road Syrah, Santa Barbara

Father's Day Dinner

Cheesy Crab Meat Cups

Marinated Flank Steak

Balsamic Potato Salad

Grilled Corn Salad

Buttermilk-Glazed Carrot Cake

*2005 Tobacco Road Cabernet Sauvignon
    "Vitality," Napa Valley*

July 4th Bash

Seven-Layer Mexican Dip

Spice-Rubbed Baby Back Ribs

Ultimate Baked Beans

Red, White and Blue Salad

Easy Peach Cobbler

Cracked Sugar Cookies

2006 Tobacco Road Syrah, Santa Barbara

Picnic at Regency Park

Marinated Shrimp and Avocado Salad

Smoked Turkey Wraps

Cucumber Scallion Salad

Best-Ever Chocolate Chip Cookies

Farmers' Market Dinner

Shrimp and Avocado Gazpacho

Balsamic-Glazed Steaks

Tomato Zucchini Tart

Fresh Plum Cake

*2005 Tobacco Road Cabernet Sauvignon
    "The Tradition," Napa Valley*

Baked Blueberry Pecan French Toast

French Toast
1 (24-inch) baguette
3 cups milk
6 eggs
1 teaspoon vanilla extract
3/4 cup packed brown sugar
1/2 teaspoon freshly grated nutmeg
1 cup pecans (about 3 ounces)
1 teaspoon unsalted butter
1/4 teaspoon salt

2 cups blueberries (about 12 ounces)
1/4 cup (1/2 stick) unsalted butter,
    cut into small pieces
1/4 cup packed brown sugar

Blueberry Syrup
1 cup blueberries (about 6 ounces)
1/2 cup pure maple syrup
1 tablespoon fresh lemon juice

To prepare the French toast, cut the baguette into twenty 1-inch slices and arrange in a single layer in a buttered 9x13-inch baking dish. Whisk the milk, eggs and vanilla in a bowl until blended. Add 3/4 cup brown sugar and the nutmeg and whisk until combined. Pour evenly over the bread. Chill, covered, for 8 to 24 hours or until all of the liquid is absorbed.

Spread the pecans in a single layer in a shallow baking pan. Place the baking pan on the middle oven rack of a preheated 350-degree oven. Toast for 8 minutes or until the pecans are fragrant. Increase the oven temperature to 400 degrees.

Add 1 teaspoon butter and the salt to the pecans and toss to coat. Sprinkle the pecans and blueberries over the chilled layer. Heat 1/4 cup butter and 1/4 cup brown sugar in a small saucepan until the butter melts, stirring occasionally. Drizzle over the prepared layers and bake for 20 minutes, or until any liquid from the blueberries is bubbling.

To prepare the syrup, combine the blueberries and maple syrup in a small saucepan. Cook over medium heat for 3 minutes or until the blueberries burst. Pour the syrup through a sieve into a heatproof pitcher, pressing on the solids with a spoon; discard the solids. Stir in the lemon juice. Serve warm with the French toast. The syrup may be prepared up to one day in advance and stored, covered, in the refrigerator. Reheat before serving.

Serves 6

Blueberry Muffin Coffee Cake

Coffee Cake
2 cups cake flour
2 teaspoons baking powder
1/2 teaspoon salt
2 cups sugar
1/2 cup (1 stick) butter (do not use margarine)
2 eggs
1 teaspoon grated lemon zest
1/2 cup half-and-half
1 teaspoon vanilla extract
2 cups fresh blueberries

Crumb Topping
1/2 cup sugar
1/3 cup all-purpose flour
1 teaspoon cinnamon
1/4 cup (1/2 stick) butter
1/2 cup chopped nuts (optional)

To prepare the coffee cake, reserve 1 teaspoon of the cake flour. Sift the remaining cake flour, the baking powder and salt together. Reserve 1 teaspoon of the sugar. Beat the remaining sugar and the butter in a mixing bowl until creamy. Add the eggs and lemon zest and mix well. Add the dry ingredients and beat until blended. Blend in the half-and-half and vanilla. The batter will be stiff.

Toss the blueberries with the reserved 1 teaspoon flour and the reserved 1 teaspoon sugar in a bowl to coat. Fold the blueberries into the batter; be careful not to break any of the blueberries. Spread the batter in a buttered and floured 10-inch bundt pan.

To prepare the topping, mix the sugar, flour and cinnamon in a bowl and cut in the butter until crumbly. Stir in the nuts. Sprinkle the topping over the prepared layer. Bake in a preheated 375-degree oven for 45 minutes. Cool in the pan for 10 minutes. Invert onto a wire rack. Invert again so the topping is on the top.

You may substitute thawed frozen blueberries for the fresh blueberries, but fresh are best.

Serves 16

Lemon Raspberry Muffins

2 1/2 cups all-purpose flour
1 cup sugar
2 1/2 teaspoons baking powder
1/4 teaspoon salt
1 cup buttermilk
2 eggs, lightly beaten
1/4 cup (1/2 stick) butter, melted
1 teaspoon vanilla extract
1/4 teaspoon lemon extract
1/2 pint fresh raspberries
2 teaspoons grated lemon zest
2 tablespoons sugar

Sift the flour, 1 cup sugar, the baking powder and salt into a large bowl and mix well. Make a well in center of the flour mixture using a large wooden spoon. Add the buttermilk, eggs, butter and flavorings to the well and mix just until moistened. Fold the raspberries and 1 teaspoon of the lemon zest into the batter.

Spoon the batter into twelve greased or paper-lined muffin cups. Mix the remaining 1 teaspoon lemon zest and 2 tablespoons sugar in a small bowl and sprinkle over the tops of the muffins. Bake in a preheated 400-degree oven for 20 minutes or until golden brown. Cool in the pan for 2 minutes. Remove to a wire rack.

Makes 1 dozen muffins

Raging Crescent Rolls

1 (8-count) can crescent rolls
4 ounces cream cheese, softened
4 slices bacon, crisp-cooked and crumbled
1/2 cup (2 ounces) shredded Cheddar cheese

Unroll the crescent roll dough and separate into eight triangles. Spread the cream cheese on one side of each triangle and sprinkle with the bacon. Roll using the package directions to form crescents.

Arrange the crescents on a baking sheet and sprinkle with the Cheddar cheese. Bake in a preheated 350-degree oven for 10 to 13 minutes or until light brown. Serve as a roll or cut into pieces and serve as an appetizer.

Makes 8 rolls

Caprese Skewers

1 tablespoon balsamic vinegar
1 tablespoon extra-virgin olive oil
1/8 teaspoon pepper
1/8 teaspoon kosher salt
4 ounces fresh mozzarella cheese, cut into 24 (1/2-inch) cubes
1 teaspoon extra-virgin olive oil
1/8 teaspoon pepper
Kosher salt to taste
24 small red cherry tomatoes or yellow grape tomatoes
24 small to medium fresh basil leaves

Whisk the vinegar, 1 tablespoon olive oil, 1/8 teaspoon pepper and 1/8 teaspoon salt in a bowl until combined. Toss the cheese with 1 teaspoon olive oil and 1/8 teaspoon pepper in a bowl to coat. Season with salt to taste.

Thread one tomato on a 5-inch bamboo skewer. Fold one basil leaf in half and slide onto the skewer. End with a cube of cheese. Repeat the process with the remaining tomatoes, remaining basil leaves and remaining cheese cubes. Brush with the vinaigrette. Arrange on a serving platter and serve immediately.

The vinaigrette may be prepared up to three days in advance and stored, covered, in the refrigerator.

Makes 24 skewers

Seven-Layer Mexican Dip

1 (16-ounce) can fat-free refried beans
1 envelope low-salt taco seasoning mix
1 cup guacamole
1 cup sour cream
1 1/2 cups (6 ounces) shredded sharp Cheddar cheese
1 cup chopped cherry tomatoes
1 fresh jalapeño chile, seeded and minced
1/4 cup chopped cilantro

Mix the beans with one-half of the taco seasoning in a small bowl. Spread over the surface of a 13-inch platter. Spread the guacamole over the bean mixture, leaving a small border of the beans exposed.

Combine the sour cream with the remaining taco seasoning in a small bowl and mix well. Spread over the prepared layers, leaving a small border of the guacamole exposed. Sprinkle with the cheese, tomatoes, jalapeño chile and cilantro in the order listed. Chill, covered, for 1 to 2 hours. Serve with tortilla chips.

Serves 8 to 10

Mango Salsa

3 cups chopped fresh mangoes
   (about 2 or 3)
1/4 cup finely chopped red onion
1 tablespoon minced seeded
   jalapeño chile

3 tablespoons chopped cilantro
1 tablespoon rice wine vinegar
1 teaspoon lemon juice
1 garlic clove, minced

Combine the mangoes, onion, jalapeño chile, cilantro, vinegar, lemon juice and garlic in a bowl and mix well. Chill, covered, for 1 hour. Serve with tortilla chips.

You can substitute peaches for the mangoes if they are not in season. Also great served over grilled fish.

Makes 3 cups

Marinated Shrimp

1/2 cup fresh lemon juice
1/4 cup vegetable oil
1/4 cup chopped parsley
2 garlic cloves, minced
1 tablespoon dry mustard
1 tablespoon salt
1 tablespoon red wine vinegar

1 bay leaf, crumbled
Dash of cayenne pepper
2 pounds peeled cooked shrimp
1 lemon, thinly sliced
1 red onion, thinly sliced
1 cup pitted black olives

Combine the lemon juice, oil, parsley, garlic, dry mustard, salt, vinegar, bay leaf and cayenne pepper in a small bowl and mix well. Combine the shrimp, lemon slices, onion and olives in a large bowl and mix well. Add the lemon juice mixture and toss to coat.

Marinate, covered, in the refrigerator for several hours, but not overnight, stirring occasionally. Serve with wooden picks.

Serves 8

Skewered Flank Steak

1 pound flank steak
3/4 cup vegetable oil
1/2 cup dry red wine
1/4 cup soy sauce
2 tablespoons lemon juice
1 tablespoon Worcestershire sauce
1 tablespoon dry mustard
1 tablespoon chopped fresh parsley
1 1/2 teaspoons freshly ground pepper

Cut the steak across the grain into 1-inch strips. Place in a shallow dish. Whisk the oil, wine, soy sauce, lemon juice, Worcestershire sauce, dry mustard, parsley and pepper in a bowl until combined and pour over the steak, turning to coat.

Marinate, covered, in the refrigerator for 2 to 10 hours, stirring occasionally. Thread the steak on metal skewers, discarding the marinade. Broil or grill the skewers for 3 minutes per side for medium-rare or until the desired degree of doneness.

Serves 8

Creole Chicken Cakes with Rémoulade Sauce

Chicken Cakes
2 tablespoons butter
1/2 red bell pepper, chopped
4 green onions, thinly sliced
1 garlic clove, crushed
3 cups chopped cooked chicken
1 cup soft bread crumbs
1 egg, lightly beaten
2 tablespoons mayonnaise
1 tablespoon Creole mustard
2 teaspoons Creole seasoning
1/4 cup vegetable oil

Rémoulade Sauce
1 cup mayonnaise
2 tablespoons Creole mustard
1 1/2 tablespoons chili sauce
2 green onions, thinly sliced
2 garlic cloves, crushed
1 tablespoon chopped fresh parsley
1/4 teaspoon ground red pepper

To prepare the cakes, melt the butter in a large skillet over medium heat. Add the bell pepper, green onions and garlic and sauté for 3 to 4 minutes or until the vegetables are tender. Combine the bell pepper mixture, chicken, bread crumbs, egg, mayonnaise, Creole mustard and Creole seasoning in a bowl and mix well.

Shape into eight 1-inch cakes to serve as an appetizer, or four 3-inch cakes to serve as an entrée. Fry the chicken cakes in the oil in a large skillet over medium heat for 3 minutes on each side or until golden brown. Drain on paper towels.

To prepare the sauce, combine the mayonnaise, Creole mustard and chili sauce in a bowl and mix well. Stir in the green onions, garlic, parsley and red pepper. Serve with the chicken cakes. Store any leftover sauce in the refrigerator.

Makes 8 appetizer cakes or 4 entrée cakes

Cheesy Crab Meat Cups

24 won ton wrappers
8 ounces cream cheese, softened
1 cup (4 ounces) shredded Swiss cheese
1/4 cup (1 ounce) grated Parmesan cheese
1 pound back-fin crab meat, shells removed and
    crab meat flaked
2 teaspoons Worcestershire sauce
1 teaspoon Old Bay seasoning
1 teaspoon hot red pepper sauce
Salt and pepper to taste
Old Bay seasoning to taste

Spray twenty-four miniature muffin cups with nonstick cooking spray. Fit the wrappers into the prepared muffin cups. Bake in a preheated 350-degree oven for 5 to 8 minutes or until golden brown. Remove to a wire rack to cool slightly. Maintain the oven temperature.

Beat the cream cheese in a bowl until smooth using a wooden spoon. Fold in the Swiss cheese and Parmesan cheese. Fold in the crab meat, Worcestershire sauce, 1 teaspoon Old Bay seasoning and the hot sauce. Season with salt and pepper.

Spoon evenly into the won ton cups and arrange the cups on a baking sheet. Sprinkle with Old Bay seasoning to taste. Bake for 10 to 15 minutes or until the filling is bubbly. Serve warm or at room temperature.

For a more crisp cup, substitute phyllo shells for the won ton wrappers.

Makes 2 dozen cups

For Cheesy Crab Meat Dip, spoon the crab meat mixture into a baking dish and bake in a preheated 350-degree oven until bubbly. Serve with assorted chips and/or crackers.

Grilled Ginger Shrimp

1 1/2 pounds large (15-count) shrimp, peeled
    and deveined with tails
1 tablespoon canola oil
2 teaspoons grated fresh ginger
1 garlic clove, minced
1/2 teaspoon salt
1 tablespoon canola oil
1 small white onion, chopped
2 teaspoons grated fresh ginger
1 garlic clove, minced
1/2 teaspoon crushed red pepper flakes
1/4 cup apricot jam
2 tablespoons soy sauce
1 tablespoon rice wine vinegar
1/2 teaspoon dark sesame oil
Hot cooked rice

Combine the shrimp, 1 tablespoon canola oil, 2 teaspoons ginger, 1 garlic clove and the salt in a bowl and toss to coat. Marinate, covered, in the refrigerator for 1 hour, stirring occasionally.

Heat 1 tablespoon canola oil in a skillet over medium heat and add the onion. Sauté for 4 to 5 minutes or until the onion is tender. Stir in 2 teaspoons ginger, 1 garlic clove and the red pepper flakes. Sauté for 2 minutes. Add the jam, soy sauce, vinegar and sesame oil and mix well. Cook for 2 to 3 minutes or until the mixture thickens and is of a sauce consistency, stirring constantly. Strain into a bowl, discarding the solids.

Drain the shrimp, discarding the marinade. Thread the shrimp on metal skewers. Grill over hot coals until the shrimp turn pink, brushing with the sauce occasionally. Serve over hot cooked rice for a main entrée.

Makes 8 to 12 appetizer servings or 4 to 6 entrée servings

Chicken Lettuce Wraps

1 pound boneless skinless chicken breasts, chopped
1/3 cup chicken broth
1 (8-ounce) can water chestnuts, drained
    and finely minced
1 small red onion, minced
3 green onions, minced
3 tablespoons minced fresh ginger
3 tablespoons minced garlic
3 tablespoons lime juice
2 tablespoons Thai fish sauce
2 tablespoons soy sauce
2 tablespoons minced red bell pepper
1 tablespoon crushed red pepper flakes
1/2 cup salted dry roasted peanuts
Lettuce leaves (red leaf, green leaf or Boston)

Process the chicken in a food processor until minced. Heat the broth in a large skillet over medium heat for 1 minute. Add the chicken and cook for 5 minutes or until the chicken is cooked through, stirring frequently. Remove from the heat.

Add the water chestnuts, red onion, green onions, ginger and garlic to the chicken and mix well. Stir in the lime juice, fish sauce, soy sauce, bell pepper and red pepper flakes. Mix in the peanuts. To serve, place a spoonful of the chicken mixture in the center of each lettuce leaf and wrap the leaf around the filling. Serve immediately.

This dish may also be prepared omitting the lettuce leaves and serving the chicken over hot cooked rice.

Serves 8

Smoked Turkey Wraps

2 tablespoons olive oil
2 large sweet onions, chopped
1 tablespoon sugar
1 teaspoon balsamic vinegar
2 (6-ounce) packages garlic and herb
    cheese spread, softened
8 (10-inch) whole grain wraps
1 1/2 pounds smoked turkey, thinly sliced
16 slices bacon, crisp-cooked and crumbled
4 cups mixed baby salad greens

Heat the olive oil in a large skillet over medium-high heat. Add the onions and sugar and sauté for 20 minutes or until the onions are caramelized. Stir in the vinegar.

Spread the cheese over each wrap and top with equal portions of the caramelized onions, turkey, bacon and salad greens.

Roll tightly to enclose the filling and wrap individually in baking parchment. Chill in the refrigerator. Cut each wrap into halves to serve.

Serves 8

Short on time? Cover cream cheese with julienned oil-pack sun-dried tomatoes. This easy and elegant appetizer is a true crowd pleaser.

Jammin' Turkey Sandwiches

Cashew Butter
2 cups unsalted roasted cashews
2 to 3 tablespoons vegetable oil
2 teaspoons sugar (optional)
1/4 teaspoon salt

Sandwiches
8 slices whole wheat focaccia bread, or
    any hearty bread
6 to 8 tablespoons good-quality raspberry preserves
8 ounces deli smoked turkey breast, thinly sliced
4 slices Havarti cheese
Mixed salad greens

To prepare the butter, process the cashews, 2 tablespoons of the oil, the sugar and salt in a food processor or blender on high speed for 30 seconds. Scrape the side of the bowl with a rubber spatula and process to a smoother consistency if desired, adding 1 tablespoon oil 1 teaspoon at a time. Taste and adjust the seasonings. Store in an airtight container in the refrigerator until serving time.

To prepare the sandwiches, spread some of the cashew butter on one side of each of four slices of the bread. Spread the desired amount of the preserves on one side of the remaining four slices of bread and layer with the turkey, cheese and greens. Top with the remaining bread slices cashew butter side down. Serve immediately.

Substitute commercially prepared cashew butter, found in natural food stores and in some supermarkets, for the homemade cashew butter, if desired.

Makes 4 sandwiches

Shrimp and Avocado Gazpacho

2 (28-ounce) cans fire-roasted diced tomatoes
4 large ripe tomatoes, finely chopped
2 cucumbers, peeled, seeded and finely chopped
1 red bell pepper, seeded and finely chopped
1/4 cup olive oil
2 tablespoons chopped fresh cilantro
1 tablespoon Worcestershire sauce
1 tablespoon sherry vinegar
2 teaspoons salt
1 teaspoon coarsely ground black pepper
1 teaspoon celery seeds
1/2 teaspoon cayenne pepper
8 ounces deveined peeled boiled shrimp
2 avocados, chopped
Juice of 1/2 large lime

Combine the canned tomatoes, fresh tomatoes, cucumbers, bell pepper and olive oil in a large glass bowl and mix gently. Stir in the cilantro, Worcestershire sauce, vinegar, salt, black pepper, celery seeds and cayenne pepper.

Chill, covered, for 6 to 8 hours, stirring occasionally. Taste and adjust the seasonings. Stir in the shrimp and avocados. Add the lime juice and mix well. Chill, covered, until serving time. Ladle into mugs or bowls and garnish with additional chopped fresh cilantro.

Makes 12 appetizer servings or 6 entrée servings

Asian Salad with Sesame Ginger Dressing

Sesame Ginger Dressing

2¹/₂ tablespoons rice wine vinegar
2 tablespoons light olive oil
2 tablespoons fresh tangerine juice
1 tablespoon dark sesame oil
2 teaspoons grated fresh ginger
1 teaspoon soy sauce
1 teaspoon minced tangerine zest
¹/₄ teaspoon salt

Salad

1 bunch spring onions
2 cups finely shredded purple cabbage
2 cups finely shredded savoy or napa cabbage
6 to 8 cups mixed salad greens
1 red, orange or yellow bell pepper, thinly sliced
1 cup shredded carrots
¹/₂ cup mung bean sprouts (optional)
¹/₂ to 1 cup peanuts or almonds (optional)

To prepare the dressing, whisk the vinegar, olive oil, tangerine juice, sesame oil, ginger, soy sauce, tangerine zest and salt in a bowl until emulsified.

To prepare the salad, thinly slice the spring onions lengthwise into 2-inch lengths. Toss the onions, cabbage, salad greens, bell pepper and carrots in a bowl. Add just enough of the dressing to coat and mix well. Sprinkle with the bean sprouts and peanuts and toss. Serve immediately.

Serves 8 to 10

A colorful and pretty addition to a dinner party buffet. The salad stays crunchy for some time even after being dressed. Makes a great light summer meal when topped with grilled steak or grilled chicken.

Thai Cabbage Salad

Thai Dressing

1/3 cup vegetable oil
1/3 cup white wine vinegar or rice vinegar
3 tablespoons sugar
3 tablespoons soy sauce
2 tablespoons chopped fresh cilantro
4 garlic cloves, minced
2 jalapeño chiles, seeded and finely chopped
1 teaspoon sweet chili sauce

Salad

1 head cabbage, shredded
1 cucumber, peeled, seeded and chopped
1 carrot, grated
1 cup roasted peanuts, coarsely chopped
5 spring onions, thinly sliced
1/2 red bell pepper, thinly sliced
1 tablespoon chopped fresh cilantro

To prepare the dressing, combine the oil, vinegar, sugar, soy sauce, cilantro, garlic, jalapeño chiles and chili sauce in a large liquid measuring cup and whisk until the sugar dissolves.

To prepare the salad, combine the cabbage, cucumber and carrot in a sealable plastic bag. Add the dressing and seal tightly. Shake to coat.

Marinate in the refrigerator for 2 hours or longer, turning occasionally. Just before serving, place the cabbage mixture in a large salad bowl. Add the peanuts, spring onions, bell pepper and cilantro and toss to combine.

Serves 8

Grilled Corn Salad

1/2 cup olive oil
2 tablespoons apple cider vinegar
1 large shallot, finely chopped
6 ears of fresh corn, husked and silk removed
1/4 cup olive oil
Salt and pepper to taste
2 cups frozen baby lima beans
2 cups teardrop, grape or cherry tomato halves
1 cup pitted kalamata olive halves
1 cup (4 ounces) coarsely grated Parmesan cheese

Whisk 1/2 cup olive oil, the vinegar and shallot in a bowl until combined. Brush the corn with 1/4 cup olive oil and sprinkle with salt and pepper. Grill over hot coals for about 10 minutes, or roast, tightly wrapped in foil, in a preheated 425-degree oven for 30 minutes. Cool slightly and then cut the corn kernels into a bowl using a sharp knife.

Cook the beans in boiling salted water in a saucepan for 10 minutes. Drain and rinse with cold water. Combine the corn, beans, tomatoes and olives in a bowl and mix well. Add the vinaigrette and toss to coat. Season with salt and pepper and sprinkle with the cheese. Serve at room temperature or chilled.

Serves 6 to 8

*E*ncourage your children to eat more vegetables by making a pact to try one new vegetable a week. Try sugar snap peas as they are sweet and taste like candy. Toss with a little sesame oil and sprinkle with sesame seeds and sea salt. Who could resist?

Cucumber Scallion Salad

1/2 cup white vinegar
3 tablespoons sugar
1 tablespoon olive oil
1/2 teaspoon red pepper flakes
1/4 teaspoon salt
2 cups grape tomatoes
1 pound Kirby or English cucumbers, peeled and chopped
1 cup thinly sliced scallions (green and white portions)
4 ounces feta cheese, crumbled

Combine the vinegar, sugar, olive oil, red pepper flakes and salt in a jar with a tight-fitting lid and seal tightly. Shake to mix.

Slice the tomatoes into halves into a bowl, catching the juices. Add the cucumbers and scallions and mix gently. Add the dressing and toss to coat. Chill, tightly covered, for 4 to 12 hours. Stir and sprinkle with the cheese just before serving.

Serves 8

Red, White and Blue Salad

Honey Dijon Vinaigrette
$1/2$ cup good-quality balsamic vinegar
$1/4$ cup clover honey
3 tablespoons Dijon mustard
2 garlic cloves, minced
1 large shallot, minced
$1/4$ teaspoon salt
$1/4$ teaspoon pepper
1 cup extra-virgin olive oil

Salad
5 ounces mixed baby salad greens
1 cup drained canned mandarin oranges,
    patted dry
1 cup sliced fresh strawberries
$1/2$ cup fresh blueberries
$1/2$ cup chopped walnuts or pecans
4 ounces blue cheese, crumbled
Grilled steak or grilled chicken breast, sliced (optional)

To prepare the dressing, whisk the vinegar, honey, Dijon mustard, garlic, shallot, salt and pepper in a bowl until combined. Add the olive oil gradually, whisking constantly until emulsified.

To prepare the salad, arrange the desired amount of greens on each salad plate. Top evenly with the mandarin oranges, strawberries and blueberries. Sprinkle with the walnuts and blue cheese. Drizzle with the vinaigrette and top with grilled steak or grilled chicken. Serve immediately.

This vinaigrette also makes a great marinade for chicken.

Serves 4 to 6

Balsamic Potato Salad

  2 pounds potatoes
  1 cup mayonnaise
  2 tablespoons balsamic vinegar
  1 1/2 teaspoons salt
  1 teaspoon sugar
  1/4 teaspoon freshly ground pepper
  1 cup chopped celery
  1/2 cup chopped yellow onion
  2 hard-cooked eggs, chopped

Cook the potatoes in enough water to cover in a saucepan until tender; drain. Cool slightly, peel and coarsely chop. Whisk the mayonnaise, vinegar, salt, sugar and pepper in a bowl until combined.

Combine the potatoes, celery, onion and eggs in a large bowl. Add the mayonnaise mixture and mix gently to coat. Chill, covered, for 2 hours or longer before serving.

Serves 8 to 12

*M*ayonnaise-based potato salads can be a problem in southern heat. Try grilling partially cooked potato slices until golden and tender, cutting into strips, and tossing with purchased Champagne vinaigrette. Easy, delicious, and will not spoil in the southern sun.

Chinese Chicken Salad

2 (3-ounce) packages beef-flavor ramen noodles
    with seasoning packets
1/2 cup slivered almonds
2 tablespoons sesame seeds
2 tablespoons vegetable oil
4 cups finely chopped cabbage
2 cups chopped cooked chicken
1/4 cup finely chopped green onions
1/2 cup vegetable oil
1/2 cup rice vinegar
5 teaspoons sugar

Break the noodles. Stir-fry the noodles, seasoning mix, almonds and sesame seeds in 2 tablespoons oil in a large skillet until brown; drain. Place the noodle mixture in a large bowl. Add the cabbage, chicken and green onions and mix well.

Whisk 1/2 cup oil, the vinegar and sugar in a bowl until the sugar dissolves. Pour over the salad and toss to coat. Chill, covered, in the refrigerator until cold.

A favorite menu item served at Faculty and Staff Appreciation Luncheons.

Serves 8

Originally published in *Raving Recipes.*

Marinated Shrimp and Avocado Salad

Lime Vinaigrette
1/2 cup fresh lime juice
1/4 cup honey
1 large garlic clove, crushed
1/2 teaspoon salt
1/4 teaspoon pepper
1/3 cup olive oil

Salad
1 pound peeled cooked large shrimp
2 avocados, chopped
1 cup fresh or thawed frozen corn kernels
1/4 cup chopped cilantro
2 tablespoons chopped red onion
Leafy salad greens

To prepare the vinaigrette, whisk the lime juice, honey, garlic, salt and pepper in a bowl until combined. Add the olive oil gradually, whisking constantly until emulsified.

To prepare the salad, combine the shrimp, avocados, corn, cilantro and onion in a large bowl and mix gently. Add the vinaigrette and mix gently. Chill, covered, for 1 hour or longer. Serve over a bed of leafy salad greens.

Serves 6 to 8

For variety, serve in martini glasses as a first course or wrap the shrimp mixture in a tortilla for a sandwich. Or, cut the shrimp into bite-size pieces and serve as a dip with corn chips or corn chip scoops.

Graduation

Marinated Flank Steak

1/4 cup soy sauce
1/4 cup vegetable oil
1/4 cup ketchup
2 teaspoons wine vinegar
1 garlic clove, minced
1 teaspoon grated fresh ginger (optional)
2 pounds flank steak
Salt and pepper to taste

Whisk the soy sauce, oil, ketchup, vinegar, garlic and ginger in a bowl until combined. Place the steak in a sealable plastic bag and pour the soy sauce mixture over the steak. Seal tightly and turn to coat.

Marinate in the refrigerator for 8 to 10 hours, turning occasionally. Let stand at room temperature for 30 minutes. Drain, discarding the marinade.

Season the steak with salt and pepper. Grill over medium-high heat to the desired degree of doneness. Let rest for 5 minutes before slicing crosswise against the grain. Flank steak is best if cooked medium-rare to medium.

Serves 4 to 6

Balsamic-Glazed Steaks

4 (6-ounce) beef steaks, 3/4 inch thick
    (such as rib-eye or strip)
Salt and pepper to taste
4 teaspoons olive oil
2/3 cup minced shallots
4 teaspoons minced fresh rosemary
6 tablespoons balsamic vinegar

Season the steaks on both sides with salt and pepper. Grill over hot coals to the desired degree of doneness. Remove the steaks to a platter and tent with foil to keep warm.

Heat the olive oil in a skillet over medium-low heat and add the shallots and rosemary. Cook for 2 minutes, stirring occasionally. Stir in the vinegar and cook for 1 minute or until the mixture is reduce to a glaze consistency. Add the accumulated juices from the steaks and mix well. Drizzle the glaze over the steaks and serve immediately.

Serves 4

Grilled Honey-Soy Pork Loin

$1/2$ cup vegetable oil
$1/3$ cup lime juice
$1/4$ cup honey
$1/4$ cup soy sauce
6 garlic cloves, minced
1 (2- to 3-pound) boneless pork loin
Salt and pepper to taste

Combine the oil, lime juice, honey, soy sauce and garlic in a bowl and mix well. Pierce the surface of the pork with a fork and place in a shallow dish. Pour the lime juice mixture over the pork and turn to coat. Marinate, covered, in the refrigerator for 8 to 10 hours, turning occasionally. Drain, discarding the marinade.

Season the pork with salt and pepper. Grill over medium-low heat for 1 hour or until a meat thermometer registers 160 degrees for medium. Let stand for 5 to 10 minutes before slicing.

Serve warm or at room temperature.

Serves 4 to 6

$\mathcal{A}$ nice choice for a buffet. You may substitute pork tenderloin for the pork loin, but the grilling time will decrease.

Spice-Rubbed Baby Back Ribs

2 tablespoons paprika
1 teaspoon garlic salt
1 teaspoon onion salt
1/2 teaspoon pepper
1/4 to 1/2 teaspoon ground cumin
1/4 to 1/2 teaspoon chili powder
1/4 teaspoon seasoned salt
2 slabs well-marbled baby back ribs
Barbecue sauce

Combine the paprika, garlic salt, onion salt, pepper, cumin, chili powder and seasoned salt in a small bowl and mix with a fork or small whisk. Rub the spice mixture over the surface of the slabs and wrap in heavy-duty foil like an envelope.

Arrange the foil-wrapped slabs in a shallow roasting pan or broiler pan. Bake in a preheated 325-degree oven for 2 hours. Spread barbecue sauce over the slabs and bake, uncovered, for 15 minutes longer or grill over hot coals for a few minutes.

Serves 4

Lemon Herb-Grilled Chicken and Vegetable Kabobs

2 to 2½ pounds chicken pieces
   (preferably with skin and bones)
¾ cup vegetable oil
¾ cup lemon juice
2 teaspoons seasoned salt
2 tablespoons chopped fresh basil, or
   2 teaspoons dried basil
2 tablespoons chopped fresh thyme,
   or 2 teaspoons dried thyme

2 teaspoons paprika
2 garlic cloves, minced
1 sweet onion, cut into 1-inch chunks
1 zucchini, cut into 1-inch chunks
Whole mushrooms
1 large green bell pepper, cut into
   1-inch chunks
Cherry tomatoes

Place the chicken in a large sealable plastic bag. Whisk the oil, lemon juice, seasoned salt, basil, thyme, paprika and garlic in a bowl until combined and pour over the chicken. Seal tightly and turn to coat. Marinate in the refrigerator for 8 to 10 hours, turning occasionally. Drain, reserving the marinade.

Alternately thread equal portions of the onion, zucchini, mushrooms, bell pepper and tomatoes on four skewers. Boil the reserved marinade in a saucepan for 5 minutes.

Grill or broil the chicken and vegetable kabobs, basting frequently with the reserved marinade. Grill the vegetables for 5 to 8 minutes per side or to the desired degree of doneness. Grill the chicken for 15 to 20 minutes per side or until cooked through. Bring any remaining reserved marinade to a boil in a saucepan and boil for 2 minutes. Arrange the chicken and the vegetable kabobs on a serving platter and drizzle with the warm marinade. Serve with hot cooked brown rice.

Serves 4

No time to make kabobs? Try this quick-and-easy tip. Toss slices of green and yellow squash in Italian salad dressing and marinate for 30 minutes. Grill until tender-crisp.

Spicy Tuna Teriyaki

4 (5- to 7-ounce) tuna steaks
2/3 cup teriyaki marinade
2 to 3 tablespoons brown sugar
2 tablespoons vegetable oil
2 garlic cloves, minced
3/4 teaspoon crushed red pepper flakes
Salt and black pepper to taste

Place the tuna in a large sealable plastic bag. Whisk the teriyaki marinade, brown sugar, oil, garlic and red pepper flakes in a nonreactive bowl until combined and pour over the tuna. Seal tightly and turn to coat. Marinate in the refrigerator for 30 minutes to 2 hours, turning two to three times. Drain, reserving the marinade. Pat the tuna dry with paper towels. Grill over hot coals until medium-rare or to the desired degree of doneness.

Bring the reserved marinade to a boil in a saucepan. Reduce the heat and simmer for 3 to 5 minutes. Drizzle over the tuna on a serving platter and sprinkle with salt and black pepper. Garnish with two thinly sliced green onions.

Serves 4

Peppered Tuna Medallions

3 tablespoons all-purpose flour
1 teaspoon salt
1 teaspoon pepper, or to taste
1 egg
2 teaspoons fresh lemon juice
4 tuna medallions, about 1 inch thick
Vegetable oil for sautéing

Mix the flour, salt and pepper in a shallow dish. Whisk the egg and lemon juice in a shallow dish until blended. Dip the tuna in the egg mixture and coat with the seasoned flour.

Add enough oil to a large skillet to measure 1/4 inch. Heat over medium-high heat until the oil is hot but not smoking. Sauté the tuna in the hot oil for 1 to 1 1/2 minutes per side (depending on the thickness of the medallions) or until brown on both sides but pink in the center, adding additional oil as needed. Serve immediately with lemon wedges.

Serves 4

Angel Hair Pasta with Fresh Tomato Sauce

1 small garlic clove, minced
Pinch of salt
3 pounds tomatoes
2 tablespoons fresh lemon juice
1 teaspoon salt
1 teaspoon sugar
1/2 teaspoon pepper
16 ounces angel hair pasta
Salt to taste
Olive oil to taste
1/2 cup chopped fresh basil
Grated Parmigiano-Reggiano cheese

Mash the garlic with a pinch of salt in a bowl until of a paste consistency.

Coarsely chop 2 pounds of the tomatoes over a bowl, catching the juices and reserving the pulp. Peel and finely chop the remaining 1 pound tomatoes over the same bowl, catching the juices and adding the finely chopped tomatoes to the coarsely chopped tomatoes. You may process the tomatoes in a food processor, but be careful not to overprocess. The sauce should be chunky. Stir the garlic mixture, lemon juice, 1 teaspoon salt, the sugar and pepper into the tomatoes and let stand for 15 minutes or longer.

Cook the pasta in boiling salted water in a saucepan using the package directions. Drain the pasta and place in a large serving bowl. Add the tomato mixture and toss to combine. Top with a drizzle of olive oil and sprinkle with basil and cheese. Serve immediately.

The flavor is best with summer-ripened tomatoes from the farmers' market or your own backyard.

Serves 6

Cherry tomatoes are a great accompaniment to grilled steak. Try sautéing the tomatoes in some olive oil just until softened. Season with salt and pepper and fresh herbs of your choice for a quick side dish.

Million-Dollar Marinade

1 cup hoisin sauce
1 1/2 tablespoons tamari
1 1/2 tablespoons sherry vinegar
1 1/2 tablespoons rice vinegar
1 tablespoon sugar
1 scallion, finely chopped
1 1/2 tablespoons minced garlic
1 tablespoon sesame oil
1 1/2 teaspoons black bean sauce
1 1/2 teaspoons grated fresh ginger
1/4 teaspoon white pepper

Combine the hoisin sauce, tamari, sherry vinegar, rice vinegar and sugar in a bowl and whisk until the sugar dissolves. Stir in the scallion, garlic, sesame oil, bean sauce, ginger and white pepper.

Pour the marinade over beef, chicken, pork, salmon, shrimp, scallops or vegetables destined for the grill. Marinate meats and vegetables in a nonreactive dish in the refrigerator for 2 to 10 hours, turning occasionally. Marinate seafood in a nonreactive dish in the refrigerator 1 to 2 hours, depending on the thickness of the seafood.

Makes 1 1/2 cups

Grilled Asian Asparagus

2 large bunches asparagus
1/3 cup low-sodium soy sauce
1/4 cup dry sherry
1 garlic clove, minced
1/2 teaspoon black pepper
Pinch of red pepper flakes

Snap off the thick woody ends of the asparagus spears and discard. Cook the asparagus in boiling water in a saucepan for 2 minutes or until tender-crisp; drain. Plunge the asparagus in a bowl of ice water to stop the cooking process and preserve the bright green color. Let stand until cool and then drain.

Combine the soy sauce, sherry, garlic, black pepper and red pepper flakes in a large sealable plastic bag and add the asparagus. Seal tightly and shake to coat. Marinate in the refrigerator for 1 to 10 hours, turning occasionally. Drain, discarding the marinade.

Grill the asparagus over medium-high heat until some grill marks are visible, turning occasionally. Serve warm or at room temperature.

Serves 4 to 6

*P*eeled baby carrots are a great convenience item. Try them tossed in olive oil with a little maple syrup and some salt and pepper to taste. Roast until tender. Makes a delicious, easy weeknight vegetable.

Ultimate Baked Beans

1 pound lean ground beef
1 large onion, coarsely chopped
1 large green pepper, coarsely chopped
Vegetable oil for sautéing (optional)
1 (28-ounce) can pork and beans
1 (15-ounce) can light kidney beans, drained and rinsed
1 (15-ounce) can dark kidney beans, drained and rinsed
1 (15-ounce) can black beans, drained and rinsed
1 cup packed light brown sugar
1 cup ketchup
1/2 cup molasses

Brown the ground beef in a skillet, stirring until crumbly. Remove the ground beef to a bowl using a slotted spoon, reserving the pan drippings. Sauté the onion and bell pepper in the reserved pan drippings, adding oil as needed.

Add the onion mixture, pork and beans, kidney beans and black beans to the ground beef and mix well. Stir in the brown sugar, ketchup and molasses. Spoon into a 4-quart baking dish. Bake in a preheated 325-degree oven for 1 hour.

Serves 8

*O*mit the ground beef and substitute vegetarian baked beans for the pork and beans for a delicious vegetarian version.

Tomato Zucchini Tart

    1 refrigerator pie pastry
    2 teaspoons olive oil
    1 zucchini, thinly sliced
    3 plum tomatoes, sliced
    1/2 cup fresh basil, chopped
    1/3 cup freshly grated Parmesan cheese
    1/3 cup light mayonnaise
    1/2 teaspoon freshly ground pepper

Fit the pastry in a tart pan or pie plate. Bake in a preheated 450-degree oven for
10 minutes or until light brown. Let stand until cool. Reduce the oven temperature
to 425 degrees.

Heat the olive oil in a large skillet over medium-high heat. Sauté the zucchini in the
hot oil for 3 to 4 minutes or until tender. Arrange the zucchini over the bottom of the
prepared tart pan and layer with the tomatoes.

Mix the basil, cheese and mayonnaise in a bowl. Drop by spoonfuls over the prepared
layers and spread gently. Sprinkle with the pepper. Bake for 10 to 15 minutes or until
the tart is heated through and the cheese is melted.

Serves 8

Makes a wonderful summertime treat when tomatoes and zucchini are at
their best.

Lemony Rice

1/4 cup (1/2 stick) butter
1/3 cup chopped celery
1/3 cup chopped scallions
1 1/2 cups white rice
2 1/4 cups chicken broth
1 1/2 tablespoons fresh lemon juice
1 tablespoon lemon zest
1 teaspoon salt
1/8 teaspoon freshly ground pepper
1 small bay leaf
1/4 cup minced parsley

Melt the butter in a large saucepan or Dutch oven over medium-low heat. Add the celery and scallions and cook for 5 minutes or until tender. Add the rice and stir to coat. Cook for 2 minutes, stirring occasionally. Add the broth, lemon juice, lemon zest, salt, pepper and bay leaf and stir gently so as not to break up the bay leaf.

Bring to a boil and then reduce the heat to low. Simmer, covered, for 25 minutes. Discard the bay leaf. Add the parsley and toss gently to mix.

Serves 6 to 8

This is a fresh and flavorful rice dish. Great served with grilled chicken or grilled fish.

Buttermilk-Glazed Carrot Cake

Cake
All-purpose flour for dusting
2 cups all-purpose flour
2 teaspoons baking soda
2 teaspoons cinnamon
1/2 teaspoon salt
2 cups sugar
3/4 cup buttermilk
3/4 cup vegetable oil
3 eggs
2 teaspoons vanilla extract
2 cups grated carrots
1 (8-ounce) can flaked coconut
1 cup chopped pecans or walnuts

Buttermilk Glaze
1 cup sugar
1 1/2 teaspoons baking soda
1/2 cup buttermilk
1/2 cup (1 stick) butter or margarine
1 tablespoon light corn syrup
1 teaspoon vanilla extract

Cream Cheese Frosting
11 ounces cream cheese, softened
3/4 cup (1 1/2 sticks) butter or
    margarine, softened
3 cups sifted confectioners' sugar
1 1/2 teaspoons vanilla extract

To prepare the cake, line three 9-inch cake pans with waxed paper. Lightly grease the waxed paper and dust with flour. Mix 2 cups flour, the baking soda, cinnamon and salt together. Beat the sugar, buttermilk, oil, eggs and vanilla in a mixing bowl at medium speed until smooth. Add the dry ingredients and beat at low speed until blended. Fold in the carrots, coconut and pecans. Spread the batter evenly in the prepared pans. Bake in a preheated 350-degree oven for 25 to 30 minutes or until wooden picks inserted in the centers of the layers come out clean.

To prepare the glaze, mix the sugar and baking soda in a large Dutch oven. Add the buttermilk, butter and corn syrup and bring to a boil over medium-high heat. Boil for 4 minutes, stirring frequently. Remove from the heat and then stir in the vanilla. Be careful as the glaze scorches and boils over easily.

Drizzle the glaze over the hot layers. Cool in the pans on wire racks for 15 minutes. Remove the layers to the wire racks to cool completely.

To prepare the frosting, beat the cream cheese and butter in a mixing bowl at medium speed until creamy. Add the confectioners' sugar and vanilla and beat until of a spreading consistency. Spread the frosting between the layers and over the top and side of the cake. Store in the refrigerator.

Serves 12

Fresh Plum Cake

3 tablespoons brandy
2 tablespoons red currant jelly
1 pound Italian prune plums or regular plums,
    cut into halves and pitted
3/4 cup sugar
1/3 cup slivered almonds
3/4 cup unbleached all-purpose flour
1/2 teaspoon baking powder
1/4 teaspoon salt
6 tablespoons unsalted butter, cut into 6 pieces,
    softened and cooled
1 egg
1 egg yolk
1 teaspoon vanilla extract
1/2 teaspoon almond extract
Confectioners' sugar for dusting

Cook the brandy and jelly in a large nonstick skillet over medium heat for 2 to 3 minutes or until reduced to a thick syrup, stirring occasionally. Remove from the heat and arrange the plums cut side down in the syrup. Cook over medium heat for 5 minutes or until the plums release their juices and a thick syrup forms again, shaking the skillet to prevent the plums from sticking. Cool the plums in the pan for 20 minutes.

Process the sugar and almonds in a food processor until the almonds are finely ground. Add the flour, baking powder and salt and pulse to combine. Add the butter and pulse until the mixture resembles coarse sand, about ten 1-second pulses. Add the egg, egg yolk and flavorings and process for 5 seconds or until smooth, scraping the bowl once if needed. The batter will be stiff.

Spread the batter in a greased and floured 9-inch springform pan. Stir the plums to coat with the syrup and arrange the plums skin side down over the surface of the batter. Bake in a preheated 350-degree oven for 40 to 45 minutes or until a wooden pick inserted near the center comes out clean and the top is golden brown. Cool in the pan on a wire rack for 30 minutes or until warm. Remove the cake from the pan and dust with confectioners' sugar. Cut into wedges and serve. Delicious with a scoop of vanilla ice cream.

Serves 6 to 8

Milk Chocolate Chip Pound Cake

2 1/2 cups all-purpose flour
1/2 teaspoon salt
1/4 teaspoon baking soda
1 cup (2 sticks) butter, softened
1 1/2 cups sugar
4 eggs
6 (1 1/2-ounce) chocolate candy bars
1 cup buttermilk
1 cup (6 ounces) chocolate chips
1 (5-ounce) can chocolate syrup
2 teaspoons vanilla extract
Confectioners' sugar for dusting

Mix the flour, salt and baking soda together. Beat the butter in a mixing bowl until creamy. Add the sugar gradually and beat at medium speed until blended. Add the eggs one at a time, beating well after each addition.

Heat the candy bars in a double boiler or in the microwave until melted. Add to the creamed mixture and mix gently to combine. Add the dry ingredients alternately with the buttermilk, mixing just until blended after each addition. Fold in the chocolate chips, chocolate syrup and vanilla.

Spread the batter in a greased and floured 10-inch bundt pan or tube pan. Bake in a preheated 325-degree oven for 1 hour and 15 minutes. Cool in the pan for 15 minutes. Remove the cake to a wire rack to cool completely. Sift confectioners' sugar over the top.

Serves 16

Lime-Glazed Pound Cake

3 1/4 cups cake flour
1/4 teaspoon baking soda
1/4 teaspoon salt
8 ounces cream cheese, softened
1 cup (2 sticks) plus 2 tablespoons
    unsalted butter, softened
3 cups sugar
6 eggs, at room temperature
3 tablespoons fresh lime juice, at room temperature
1 teaspoon vanilla extract
2 teaspoons finely grated lime zest
3/4 cup sugar
1/4 cup fresh lime juice, at room temperature

Position the oven rack in the lower third of the oven. Sift the cake flour, baking soda and salt together. Beat the cream cheese and butter in a mixing bowl at medium speed for 30 to 40 seconds or until creamy and smooth. Add 3 cups sugar and beat for 5 minutes or until light and fluffy, scraping the bowl occasionally. Add the eggs one at a time, beating well after each addition. Beat in 3 tablespoons lime juice and the vanilla until blended. Add the flour mixture one-third at a time, beating constantly at low speed just until smooth after each addition and scraping the bowl occasionally. Fold in the lime zest.

Spread the batter in a greased and floured tube pan, mounding the outside side of the batter higher than the center side. Bake in a preheated 325-degree oven for 1 hour and 30 minutes or until golden brown. Cool in the pan on a wire rack for 10 minutes. Remove to a wire rack. Whisk 3/4 cup sugar and 1/4 cup lime juice in a bowl until the sugar dissolves. Generously brush the top and side of the warm cake with the lime glaze.

Serves 12

Best-Ever Chocolate Chip Cookies

2¼ cups all-purpose flour
1 teaspoon baking soda
1 teaspoon salt
1½ cups packed light brown sugar
1 cup (2 sticks) butter, softened
1 teaspoon vanilla extract
2 eggs
2 cups (12 ounces) semisweet chocolate chips
½ cup chocolate-covered toffee bits
1 cup chopped pecans

Sift the flour, baking soda and salt together. Cream the brown sugar, butter and vanilla in a mixing bowl until light and fluffy, scraping the bowl occasionally. Add the eggs one at a time, beating well after each addition. Add the dry ingredients gradually, beating constantly until blended. Stir in the chocolate chips, toffee bits and pecans.

Drop by tablespoonfuls 2 inches apart onto an ungreased cookie sheet lined with baking parchment. Bake in a preheated 375-degree oven for 9 to 12 minutes. The shorter baking time will yield a soft cookie and the longer baking time will yield a crisp cookie. Cool on the cookie sheet for 2 minutes. Remove to a wire rack to cool completely. Store in an airtight container.

The toffee bits add a distinct chewiness to this cookie. They are sold as Heath Bits 'O Brickle Toffee Bits or Skor English Toffee Bits.

Makes about 4 dozen cookies

Cracked Sugar Cookies

1 1/2 cups granulated sugar
1/2 cup shortening
1/2 cup (1 stick) butter or margarine
2 egg yolks
1 teaspoon baking soda
1 teaspoon cream of tartar
1/2 teaspoon vanilla extract
1/2 teaspoon lemon juice
2 cups all-purpose flour
Tinted sugar

Cream the granulated sugar, shortening and butter in a mixing bowl until light and fluffy. Add the egg yolks, baking soda, cream of tartar, vanilla and lemon juice and mix until smooth. Add the flour 1/2 cup at a time, beating until blended after each addition. Chill, covered, for several hours.

Shape the dough into balls and coat with tinted sugar. Arrange on a cookie sheet. Bake in a preheated 350-degree oven for 12 to 15 minutes or until the edges are golden brown. Cool on the cookie sheet for 2 minutes. Remove to a wire rack to cool completely. Store in an airtight container. The tops of the cookies will crack as they bake.

Makes 4 dozen cookies

Holden's Barbecue Banana Pudding

10 egg yolks
2 cups sugar
3 cups water
1 cup all-purpose flour
1 (12-ounce) can evaporated milk
1 tablespoon vanilla extract
1 (32-ounce) package vanilla wafers
7 or 8 ripe bananas, cut into 1/4-inch slices
10 egg whites, at room temperature
1/2 cup sugar

Combine the egg yolks, sugar, water, flour, evaporated milk and vanilla in a heavy saucepan. Bring to a low boil over medium heat and cook until thickened and the consistency of a custard, stirring constantly to prevent the custard from sticking or burning. Remove from the heat.

Layer the vanilla wafers, bananas and custard one-third at a time in a baking pan. Beat the egg whites in a nonreactive mixing bowl at medium-high speed until soft peaks form. Add 1/2 cup sugar a couple of tablespoons at a time, beating constantly until the sugar dissolves. Spread the meringue over the prepared layers. Bake in a preheated 325-degree oven for 15 to 20 minutes or until the meringue is light brown.

Serves 8 to 10

Holden's Barbecue, located just north of Ravenscroft in Youngsville, North Carolina, has catered Ravenscroft's Annual New Parent Barbecue, the Fine Art's Picnic, and numerous other on-campus functions for many years. Parents, faculty, and alumni always look forward to Holden's barbecue, and especially their traditional southern banana pudding.

Peach and Blueberry Compote

3/4 cup sugar
1/3 cup water
2 (2-inch) cinnamon sticks
1 teaspoon fresh lemon juice
Dash of salt
3 cups sliced fresh ripe peaches (about 8)
1 cup blueberries
Vanilla ice cream or pound cake

Combine the sugar, water, cinnamon, lemon juice and salt in a saucepan and bring to a boil, stirring occasionally. Stir in the peaches.

Cook, covered, for 10 minutes or until the peaches are tender. Remove from the heat and let stand until cool. Fold in the blueberries. Spoon into a bowl and chill, covered, in the refrigerator. Discard the cinnamon sticks. Serve the compote over vanilla ice cream or pound cake in sherbet glasses. Garnish with fresh mint leaves.

Serves 6 to 8

Need a quick-and-easy summertime dessert? Try grilling stone fruits like peaches or plums. Great served with vanilla ice cream.

Blueberry Sour Cream Cake

Crust
1 1/2 cups all-purpose flour
1 1/2 teaspoons baking powder
1/2 cup (1 stick) butter or margarine, softened
1/2 cup sugar
1 egg
1 teaspoon vanilla extract

Blueberry Filling
4 cups fresh blueberries
2 cups sour cream
2 egg yolks, lightly beaten
1/2 cup sugar
1 teaspoon vanilla extract

Whipped Cream Topping
1 1/2 cups heavy whipping cream
1/4 cup sifted confectioners' sugar

To prepare the crust, mix the flour and baking powder together. Cream the butter in a mixing bowl until light and fluffy. Add the sugar gradually, beating constantly at medium speed until blended. Beat in the egg until smooth. Add the flour mixture and mix just until blended. Stir in the vanilla. Pat the dough over the bottom of a 9-inch springform pan.

To prepare the filling, sprinkle the blueberries over the prepared layer. Combine the sour cream, egg yolks, sugar and vanilla in a bowl and mix well. Spread over the prepared layers. Bake in a preheated 350-degree oven for 1 hour or until the edge of the filling is light brown. Cool in the pan on a wire rack. Chill, covered, in the refrigerator.

To prepare the topping, beat the cream in a mixing bowl until foamy. Add the confectioners' sugar gradually, beating constantly until soft peaks form. Remove the side of the pan and place the cake on a serving plate. Spread with the topping.

This is a very good summer dessert—part cheesecake and part custard pie.

Serves 8 to 10

*T*he author, a grandparent, submitted this recipe to *Southern Living Magazine*. The recipe was published in June of 1990 in their twenty-five-year Silver Jubilee Issue.

Easy Peach Cobbler

1/2 cup (1 stick) butter
1 cup self-rising flour
1 cup sugar
1/2 teaspoon cinnamon
1 cup milk
4 cups sliced fresh or frozen peaches
1 cup sugar
1/2 teaspoon cinnamon
1/2 teaspoon nutmeg

Melt the butter in a 9×13-inch baking pan in a preheated 350-degree oven. Maintain the oven temperature. Combine the self-rising flour, 1 cup sugar, 1/2 teaspoon cinnamon and the milk in a bowl and mix well. Pour the batter in the prepared pan; do not stir.

Combine the peaches, 1 cup sugar and 1/2 teaspoon cinnamon in a 2-quart saucepan and bring to a boil, stirring occasionally. Remove from the heat and cool for 2 minutes. Pour over the prepared layers; do not stir. Bake for 40 minutes or until golden brown. Sprinkle with the nutmeg.

Serves 6 to 8

Restaurant Recipe Contributors

The Angus Barn, Ltd.
9401 Glenwood Avenue
Raleigh, North Carolina 27617
919-781-2444
http://www.angusbarn.com

Van Eure, Owner
Walter J. Royal, Executive Chef

Holden's Barbecue
582 US 1 Highway
Youngsville, North Carolina 27596
919-556-3607

Neil Holden, Owner

Second Empire Restaurant and Tavern
Dodd-Hinsdale House
330 Hillsborough Street
Raleigh, North Carolina 27603
919-829-3663
http://www.second-empire.com

Kim Reynolds '75, Owner
Daniel Schurr, Executive Chef

Winston's Grille
6401 Falls of Neuse Road
Raleigh, North Carolina 27615
919-790-0700
http://www.winstonsgrille.com

Charles Winston, Jr. '78, Owner
Wil O'Neal, Owner

Index

Accompaniments. *See also* Salsas
Blueberry Syrup, 186
Cashew Butter, 199
Cider Syrup, 20
Orange-Honey Butter, 140

Almonds
Almond Crunch, 92
Crunchy Orange Almond Salad, 113
Swiss Almond Spread, 106

Appetizers. *See also* Dips; Spreads
Caprese Skewers, 190
Cheese Krispies, 147
Cheesy Crab Meat Cups, 195
Chicken Lettuce Wraps, 197
Curried Chicken Canapés, 141
Empanadas, 27
Marinated Shrimp, 192
Marinated Vegetable Platter, 24
Pepper Jelly and Brie Tartlets, 74
Petite Potato Pancakes, 75
Pigs in Cashmere Blankets, 107
Sausage-Stuffed Mushrooms, 28
Skewered Flank Steak, 193
Spicy Won Tons, 108

Apple
Baked Apple and Cranberry Crisp, 90
Cheesy Apple Dapple Squares, 58
Company Salad with Raspberry
    Vinaigrette, 79
Old Southern Apple Cake, 90
Pumpkin Apple Streusel Muffins, 23
Sausage-Stuffed Acorn Squash, 45
Sour Cream Apple Pie, 62
Spinach, Apple and Bacon Salad, 37

Artichokes
Artichoke Cheese Spread, 142
Couscous à la Grecque, 169
Marinated Vegetable Platter, 24
Mediterranean Pasta Salad, 40

Asparagus
Chicken and Asparagus Casserole, 158
Grilled Asian Asparagus, 218
Ham and Asparagus Quiche, 138
Marinated Asparagus Salad, 150

Bacon
Bacon and Egg Puff, 137
Bacon-Stuffed Deviled Eggs, 136
Spinach, Apple and Bacon Salad, 37

Beans
Red and White Chicken Chili, 109
Red Hot Chili for a Crowd, 110
Roasted Green Beans, 166
Salmon with Tomatoes, Basil and
    White Beans, 161
Ultimate Baked Beans, 219
Vegetarian Bean Chili, 31

Beef. *See also* Ground Beef
Balsamic-Glazed Steaks, 210
Beef and Scallion Bundles, 156
Beef Bourguignon, 114
Beef Fillets with Marsala Sauce, 82
Beef Tenderloin with
    Cabernet au Jus, 81
Bourbon-Marinated Beef
    Tenderloin, 155
Burgundy Beef Tips, 114
Flank Steak in Wine Sauce, 41
Marinated Flank Steak, 209
Red Hot Chili for a Crowd, 110
Skewered Flank Steak, 193
Southern Sweet-and-Sour Brisket, 83

Biscuits
Savory Southern Biscuits, 21
Southern Biscuits, 139
Sweet Potato Angel Biscuits, 22

Blueberry
Baked Blueberry Pecan French Toast, 186
Blueberry Gelatin Salad, 149
Blueberry Muffin Coffee Cake, 187
Blueberry Sour Cream Cake, 230
Mixed Berry Pie with Pecan-Orange
    Lattice Crust, 128
Peach and Blueberry Compote, 229
Red, White and Blue Salad, 205

Breads. *See also* Biscuits; Muffins
Best-Ever White Bread, 104
Cranberry Scones with
 Orange-Honey Butter, 140
Lemon Raspberry Muffins, 188
Overnight Potato Rolls, 69
Quick Pecan Rolls, 139
Raging Crescent Rolls, 189
Sour Cream Corn Bread, 103

Breakfast/Brunch. *See also* Egg Dishes
Baked Blueberry Pecan French Toast, 186
Blueberry Muffin Coffee Cake, 187
Breakfast Spice Bread, 102
Caramelized French Toast, 70
Country Ham Rolls, 19
French Toast Strata with
 Cider Syrup, 20
Ham and Asparagus Quiche, 138
Moravian Sugar Cake, 71
Mushroom Shallot Quiche, 18
Noodle Kugel, 70
Raging Crescent Rolls, 189

Broccoli
Garlic Broccoli, 52
Mediterranean Pasta Salad, 40
Napa Cabbage Salad, 35
Pasta Primavera, 165

Cabbage
Asian Salad with Sesame Ginger
 Dressing, 201
Chinese Chicken Salad, 207
Napa Cabbage Salad, 35
Swiss Potato Soup, 111
Thai Cabbage Salad, 202

Cakes
Buttermilk-Glazed Carrot Cake, 222
Chocolate Layer Cake, 55
French Cream Cake, 173
Fresh Plum Cake, 223
Kentucky Butter Cake, 171
Lime-Glazed Pound Cake, 225
Milk Chocolate Chip Pound Cake, 224
Old Southern Apple Cake, 90

Pumpkin Pound Cake with
 Brown Sugar Glaze, 56
Red Velvet Cake, 91
White Chocolate Lemon Curd
 Layer Cake, 174

Carrots
Carrot Soufflé, 87
Honeyed Carrot Coins, 87
Mashed Turnip with Carrots and Orange, 88

Cheese
Artichoke Cheese Spread, 142
Baked Brie with Cranberries, 73
Blue Cheese Ball, 73
Blue Cheese Bow Tie Pasta Salad, 154
Blue Cheese Coleslaw, 113
Cheddar Muffins, 103
Cheese Krispies, 147
Chili Cheese Mexican Dip, 105
Classic Southern Pimento Cheese, 143
Pepper Jelly and Brie Tartlets, 74
Spicy Pimento Cheese, 25
White Cheddar au Gratin Potatoes, 88

Cheesecakes
Angus Barn Key Lime Cheesecake, 178
Cranberry Swirl Cheesecake, 129
White Chocolate Raspberry
 Cheesecake, 96

Chicken
Asian Chicken Salad with
 Peanut Dressing, 153
Blackened Chicken Cordon Bleu, 117
Cache Chicken, 159
Chicken and Asparagus Casserole, 158
Chicken, Basil and Cashew Pâté, 144
Chicken Caprese with Tomato
 Basil Sauce, 118
Chicken Lettuce Wraps, 197
Chicken Salad with Blue Cheese and
 Dried Cherries, 39
Chicken with Sun-Dried Tomato Sauce, 160
Chinese Chicken Salad, 207
Creole Chicken Cakes with
 Rémoulade Sauce, 194

Curried Chicken Canapés, 141
Empanadas, 27
Greek Chicken Breasts, 46
Lemon Herb-Grilled Chicken and
    Vegetable Kabobs, 213
Linguini with Sun-Dried Tomatoes and
    Olives, 121
Red and White Chicken Chili, 109
Roasted Chicken Salad, 38
Savory Chicken Crescents, 26
Spicy Oven-Fried Chicken, 47

Chili
Beef and Sausage Chili, 30
Red and White Chicken Chili, 109
Red Hot Chili for a Crowd, 110
Vegetarian Bean Chili, 31

Chocolate
Almond Crunch, 92
Best-Ever Chocolate Chip Cookies, 226
Chocolate Layer Cake, 55
Chocolate Strawberry Decadence, 172
Cowboy Cookies, 59
French Cream Cake, 173
Frosted Fudge Brownies, 126
Mexican Brownies, 175
Milk Chocolate Chip Pound Cake, 224
Mint Meringue Cookies, 176
Pots de Crème, 131
Red Velvet Cake, 91

Cookies
Best-Ever Chocolate Chip Cookies, 226
Cowboy Cookies, 59
Cracked Sugar Cookies, 227
Ginger Bends, 60
Holiday Snickerdoodles, 94
Mint Meringue Cookies, 176
Oatmeal Lace Cookies, 177

Cookies, Bar
Cheesy Apple Dapple Squares, 58
Cranberry Bars, 93
Frosted Fudge Brownies, 126
Mexican Brownies, 175
Molasses Bars, 57

Corn
Corn and Crab Soup, 76
Grilled Corn Salad, 203
Marinated Shrimp and Avocado Salad, 208
Sausage and Corn Chowder, 111
Sour Cream Corn Bread, 103
Tailgate Corn Chowder, 32
White Corn Risotto, 125

Crab Meat
Baked Seafood Salad, 49
Casserole Saint Jacques, 86
Cheesy Crab Meat Cups, 195
Corn and Crab Soup, 76
Crab Cakes, 163

Cranberry
Baked Apple and Cranberry Crisp, 90
Baked Brie with Cranberries, 73
Cranberry Bars, 93
Cranberry Scones with
    Orange-Honey Butter, 140
Cranberry Swirl Cheesecake, 129
Cranberry Tart, 60
Holiday Citrus Salad, 78

Desserts. See also Cakes; Cheesecakes;
    Cookies; Cookies, Bar; Pies; Sauces, Sweet
Almond Crunch, 92
Baked Apple and Cranberry Crisp, 90
Baked Pears with Blue Cheese and Port, 63
Blueberry Sour Cream Cake, 230
Chocolate Strawberry Decadence, 172
Cranberry Tart, 60
Easy Peach Cobbler, 231
Eggnog Bavarian, 97
Holden's Barbecue Banana Pudding, 228
Peach and Blueberry Compote, 229
Pots de Crème, 131
Second Empire Sweet Potato
    Bread Pudding, 130
Strawberries with
    Grand Marnier Sauce, 180

Dips
Chili Cheese Mexican Dip, 105
Seven-Layer Mexican Dip, 191

Egg Dishes
Bacon and Egg Puff, 137
Bacon-Stuffed Deviled Eggs, 136
Country Egg and Sausage Pie, 102
Three-Cheese Breakfast Strata, 68

Eggplant
Couscous à la Grecque, 169
Italian Vegetable Lasagna, 51

Fish. *See also* Salmon; Tuna
Spanish Fish, 48

Frostings/Icings
Chocolate Icing, 126
Cream Cheese Frosting, 91, 222
White Chocolate Cream Cheese Frosting, 174

Fruit. *See also* Apple; Blueberry; Cranberry;
    Orange; Peach; Pumpkin; Raspberry;
    Salads, Fruit; Strawberry
Baked Pears with Blue Cheese and Port, 63
Holden's Barbecue Banana Pudding, 228
Mango Salsa, 192

Ground Beef
Beef and Sausage Chili, 30
Ultimate Baked Beans, 219
Winston's Grille Meat Loaf, 42

Ham
Blue Cheese Bow Tie Pasta Salad, 154
Buttery Ham Spread, 145
Country Ham Rolls, 19
Ham and Asparagus Quiche, 138
Pineapple-Glazed Ham, 157

Marinade, Million-Dollar, 217

Lemon, 164, 174, 188, 213, 221

Lobster
Baked Seafood Salad, 49

Menus
ACC Tournament Party, 101
Après Ski, 101

Bridal Shower, 135
Christmas Eve Dinner, 67
Christmas Morning Brunch, 67
Derby Day, 135
Do-Ahead Halloween Dinner, 17
Easy Beach House Supper, 185
Elegant Fall Dinner, 17
Farmers' Market Dinner, 185
Father's Day Dinner, 185
Football Tailgate, 17
Graduation Celebration, 185
Home-style Hanukkah Dinner, 67
July 4th Bash, 185
Mardi Gras Party, 101
Mother's Day Luncheon, 135
Neighborhood Potluck, 17
"New" Year's Traditions, 101
Picnic at Regency Park, 185
Picnic at the Lake, 17
Ring in the New Year, 67
Romantic Valentine's Dinner, 101
Southern Easter Dinner, 135
Spring Garden Party, 135
Sunday Brunch with Friends, 17, 135
Thanksgiving Dinner, 67

Muffins
Cheddar Muffins, 103
Lemon Raspberry Muffins, 188
Pumpkin Apple Streusel Muffins, 23

Mushrooms
Italian Vegetable Lasagna, 51
Lemon Herb-Grilled Chicken and
    Vegetable Kabobs, 213
Mushroom Shallot Quiche, 18
Pasta Primavera, 165
Pasta Shells with Mushrooms and
    Radicchio, 122
Sausage-Stuffed Mushrooms, 28
Warm Balsamic Mushroom Salad, 80
Wild Mushroom Bread Pudding, 53

Nuts. *See* Almonds; Pecans

Orange
Crunchy Orange Almond Salad, 113

Holiday Citrus Salad, 78
Mashed Turnip with Carrots and Orange, 88
Orange-Honey Butter, 140
Red, White and Blue Salad, 205

Pasta. *See also* Salads, Pasta
Angel Hair Pasta with
    Fresh Tomato Sauce, 216
Easy Shrimp Pasta, 50
Italian Vegetable Lasagna, 51
Linguini with Sun-Dried Tomatoes and
    Olives, 121
Noodle Kugel, 70
Pasta Primavera, 165
Pasta Shells with Mushrooms and
    Radicchio, 122
Sausage Tortellini Soup, 34

Peach
Easy Peach Cobbler, 231
Peach and Blueberry Compote, 229

Pecans
Baked Blueberry Pecan French Toast, 186
Cowboy Cookies, 59
Old-Fashioned Pecan Pie, 61
Quick Pecan Rolls, 139

Peppers
Asian Salad with Sesame Ginger
    Dressing, 201
Country Egg and Sausage Pie, 102
Kale with Roasted Red Peppers and
    Olives, 54
Lemon Herb-Grilled Chicken and
    Vegetable Kabobs, 213
Marinated Vegetable Platter, 24
Red Hot Chili for a Crowd, 110
Shrimp and Avocado Gazpacho, 200

Pies
Butterscotch Pie, 127
Mixed Berry Pie with Pecan-Orange
    Lattice Crust, 128
Old-Fashioned Pecan Pie, 61
Pumpkin Mousse Pie, 95
Sour Cream Apple Pie, 62

Pork. *See also* Bacon; Ham; Sausage
Apricot-Glazed Pork Loin, 85
Citrus-Marinated Pork Tenderloin, 115
Gingered Pork Tenderloins, 43
Grilled Honey-Soy Pork Loin, 211
Herb-Roasted Loin of Pork, 116
North Carolina Barbecue, 116
Red Hot Chili for a Crowd, 110
Spice-Rubbed Baby Back Ribs, 212
Stuffed Pork Tenderloins, 84
Tuscan Grilled Pork, 44
Warm Pancetta, Goat Cheese and
    Spinach Salad, 152

Potatoes
Balsamic Potato Salad, 206
Moravian Sugar Cake, 71
New Potato and Chive Salad, 151
Overnight Potato Rolls, 69
Petite Potato Pancakes, 75
Sausage and Corn Chowder, 111
Swiss Potato Soup, 111
Tailgate Corn Chowder, 32
White Cheddar au Gratin
    Potatoes, 88

Poultry. *See* Chicken; Turkey

Pumpkin
Pumpkin Apple Streusel Muffins, 23
Pumpkin Mousse Pie, 95
Pumpkin Pound Cake with
    Brown Sugar Glaze, 56

Raspberry
Lemon Raspberry Muffins, 188
Mixed Berry Pie with Pecan-Orange
    Lattice Crust, 128
Raspberry Dessert Sauce, 181
White Chocolate Raspberry
    Cheesecake, 96

Rice
Apricot Rice Pilaf, 170
Lemony Rice, 221
White Corn Risotto, 125
Wild Rice Dressing, 89

Salad Dressings
Creamy Anchovy Dressing, 36
Dijon Vinaigrette, 37
Honey Dijon Vinaigrette, 205
Lemon Pesto Dressing, 24
Lime Vinaigrette, 208
Orange Dressing, 113
Peanut Dressing, 153
Raspberry Vinaigrette, 79
Sesame Ginger Dressing, 201
Soy Dressing, 35
Thai Dressing, 202

Salads, Fruit
Ambrosia, 78
Blueberry Gelatin Salad, 149
Crunchy Orange Almond Salad, 113
Holiday Citrus Salad, 78
Minted Fruit Salad, 148
Red, White and Blue Salad, 205

Salads, Main Dish
Asian Chicken Salad with Peanut Dressing, 153
Chicken Salad with Blue Cheese and
    Dried Cherries, 39
Chinese Chicken Salad, 207
Marinated Shrimp and Avocados, 208
Roasted Chicken Salad, 38

Salads, Pasta
Blue Cheese Bow Tie Pasta Salad, 154
Mediterranean Pasta Salad, 40

Salads, Vegetable
Asian Salad with Sesame Ginger
    Dressing, 201
Balsamic Potato Salad, 206
Blue Cheese Coleslaw, 113
Caesar Salad, 36
Company Salad with Raspberry
    Vinaigrette, 79
Crunchy Orange Almond Salad, 113
Cucumber Scallion Salad, 204
Grilled Corn Salad, 203
Marinated Asparagus Salad, 150
Napa Cabbage Salad, 35
New Potato and Chive Salad, 151

Red, White and Blue Salad, 205
Spinach, Apple and Bacon Salad, 37
Thai Cabbage Salad, 202
Warm Balsamic Mushroom Salad, 80
Warm Pancetta, Goat Cheese and
    Spinach Salad, 152

Salmon
Barbecued Salmon with Cucumber Salsa, 162
Salmon with Tomatoes, Basil and
    White Beans, 161
Smoked Salmon Mousse with Caviar, 146

Salsas
Cucumber Salsa, 162
Mango Salsa, 192

Sauces, Savory
Béchamel Sauce, 163
Cabernet Sauce, 81
Rémoulade Sauce, 194

Sauces, Sweet
Grand Marnier Sauce, 180
Raspberry Dessert Sauce, 181

Sausage
Beef and Sausage Chili, 30
Chili Cheese Mexican Dip, 105
Country Egg and Sausage Pie, 102
Hoppin' John, 123
Pigs in Cashmere Blankets, 107
Sausage and Corn Chowder, 111
Sausage-Stuffed Acorn Squash, 45
Sausage-Stuffed Mushrooms, 28
Sausage Tortellini Soup, 34
Spicy Won Tons, 108

Scallops
Casserole Saint Jacques, 86
Heavenly Scallops in Dijon Cream Sauce, 72
Pan-Seared Sea Scallops in Champagne
    Cream Sauce, 119
Scallops in Champagne Saffron Sauce, 29

Seafood. See Crab Meat; Lobster;
    Scallops; Shrimp

Shrimp
Baked Lemon Shrimp, 164
Baked Seafood Salad, 49
Casserole Saint Jacques, 86
Easy Shrimp Pasta, 50
Grilled Ginger Shrimp, 196
Marinated Shrimp, 192
Marinated Shrimp and Avocado Salad, 208
Shrimp and Avocado Gazpacho, 200
Shrimp and Grits Casserole, 120

Side Dishes. *See also* Rice
Cheese Grits, 120
Couscous à la Grecque, 169
Hoppin' John, 123
Onion Tart, 167
Rosemary Spoon Bread, 52
Wild Mushroom Bread Pudding, 53

Soups. *See also* Chili
Baked Onion Soup, 33
Corn and Crab Soup, 76
Roasted Tomato Soup, 112
Roasted Winter Squash Soup, 77
Sausage and Corn Chowder, 111
Sausage Tortellini Soup, 34
Shrimp and Avocado
Gazpacho, 200
Swiss Potato Soup, 111
Tailgate Corn Chowder, 32

Spinach
Company Salad with Raspberry
Vinaigrette, 79
Spinach, Apple and Bacon Salad, 37
Warm Pancetta, Goat Cheese and
Spinach Salad, 152

Spreads
Artichoke Cheese Spread, 142
Blue Cheese Ball, 73
Buttery Ham Spread, 145
Chicken, Basil and Cashew Pâté, 144
Classic Southern Pimento Cheese, 143
Lentil Pâté, 105
Orange-Honey Butter, 140
Smoked Salmon Mousse with Caviar, 146

Spicy Pimento Cheese, 25
Swiss Almond Spread, 106

Squash
Italian Vegetable Lasagna, 51
Lemon Herb-Grilled Chicken and
Vegetable Kabobs, 213
Pasta Primavera, 165
Roasted Winter Squash Soup, 77
Sausage-Stuffed Acorn Squash, 45
Tomato Zucchini Tart, 220

Strawberry
Chocolate Strawberry
Decadence, 172
Cucumber Salsa, 162
Red, White and Blue Salad, 205
Strawberries with Grand Marnier
Sauce, 180

Sweet Potatoes
Second Empire Sweet Potato
Bread Pudding, 130
Sweet Potato Angel Biscuits, 22
Sweet Potato Soufflé, 168

Tomatoes
Angel Hair Pasta with Fresh
Tomato Sauce, 216
Beef and Sausage Chili, 30
Caprese Skewers, 190
Chicken with Sun-Dried Tomato Sauce, 160
Grilled Corn Salad, 203
Italian Vegetable Lasagna, 51
Lemon Herb-Grilled Chicken and
Vegetable Kabobs, 213
Linguini with Sun-Dried Tomatoes and
Olives, 121
Marinated Vegetable Platter, 24
Pasta Primavera, 165
Red and White Chicken Chili, 109
Red Hot Chili for a Crowd, 110
Roasted Tomato Soup, 112
Salmon with Tomatoes, Basil and
White Beans, 161
Seven-Layer Mexican Dip, 191
Shrimp and Avocado Gazpacho, 200

Tomato Zucchini Tart, 220
Vegetarian Bean Chili, 31

Tuna
Peppered Tuna Medallions, 215
Spicy Tuna Teriyaki, 214

Turkey
Jammin' Turkey Sandwiches, 199
Red Hot Chili for a Crowd, 110
Smoked Turkey Wraps, 198

Vegetables. *See also* Artichokes;
Asparagus; Beans; Broccoli;
Cabbage; Carrots; Corn; Eggplant;
Mushrooms; Peppers; Potatoes;
Salads, Vegetable; Spinach; Squash;
Sweet Potatoes; Tomatoes
Kale with Roasted Red Peppers and
Olives, 54
Marinated Vegetable Platter, 24
Mashed Turnip with Carrots and
Orange, 88
Onion Tart, 167
Sautéed Collard Greens, 124

Vegetarian Entrées
Angel Hair Pasta with
Fresh Tomato Sauce, 216
Couscous à la Grecque, 169
Hoppin' John, 123
Italian Vegetable Lasagna, 51
Linguini with Sun-Dried Tomatoes and
Olives, 121
Mushroom Shallot Quiche, 18
Onion Tart, 167
Pasta Primavera, 165
Pasta Shells with Mushrooms and
Radicchio, 122
Tailgate Corn Chowder, 32
Tomato Zucchini Tart, 220
Vegetarian Bean Chili, 31
Wild Mushroom Bread Pudding, 53

Ravenscroft School is proud to present

Excellent Courses
A Culinary Legacy of Ravenscroft

To order additional copies, or for more information,
please contact Ravenscroft School at 919-847-0900, or visit
our Web site at http://excellentcourses.ravenscroft.org.

*The Ravenscroft community, guided by our legacy of
excellence, nurtures individual potential and prepares students
to thrive in a complex and interdependent world.*